Terrorism
Political Violence at Home and Abroad

Ron Fridell

Enslow Publishers, Inc.

40 Industrial Road   PO Box 38
Box 398   Aldershot
Berkeley Heights, NJ 07922   Hants GU12 6BP
USA   UK
http://www.enslow.com

Library of Congress Cataloging-in-Publication Data

Fridell, Ron.
    Terrorism : political violence at home and abroad / Ron Fridell.
       p. cm. — (Issues in focus)
    Includes bibliographical references and index.
    ISBN 0-7660-1671-4 (hardcover)
    1. Terrorism—Juvenile literature. 2. Political violence—Juvenile
literature. [1. Terrorism. 2. Political violence.] I. Title. II. Issues in
focus (Hillside, N.J.)
HV6431 .F73 2001
303.6'25—dc21

                            00-012459

To Our Readers: We have done our best to make sure all Internet
addresses in this book were active and appropriate when we went to
press. However, the author and the publisher have no control over and
assume no liability for the material available on those Internet sites or
on other Web sites they may link to. Any comments or suggestions can
be sent by e-mail to comments@enslow.com or to the address on the
back cover.

Illustration Credits: AP/Worldwide Photos, p. 80; Enslow
Publishers, Inc., pp. 11, 86; Federal Bureau of Investigation,
pp. 7, 55, 73, 77; FEMA News Photo, pp. 38, 59, 61, 66;
courtesy of Ohio State University Department of History, p. 17;
Southern Poverty Law Center, p. 19; U.S. Department of
Defense, p. 98; U.S. Navy, pp. 48, 49.

Cover Illustration: Aris Economopoulos/*The Star-Ledger*. Shown
are the twin towers of the World Trade Center in New
York City on September 11, 2001. The Statue of Liberty is in
the foreground.

Contents

1

What Is a Terrorist?

A Nissan truck rolls through the streets of Dar es Salaam in the east African nation of Tanzania. It is 10:30 A.M. on a Friday morning in August 1998. At this same moment four hundred miles north, a Mitsubishi truck rolls through the streets of Nairobi, Kenya.

These two trucks have three things in common. Both are loaded with several hundred pounds of explosives, both are driven by suicide bombers, and both are headed for an American embassy.

In Dar es Salaam, the embassy is set back from the roadway and surrounded by a two-foot-thick concrete-and-iron wall. The

Nissan truck approaches the entrance gates to the compound, but the driver must stop short. His way is blocked by a big, bulky water tanker truck making its regular 10:30 A.M. delivery.

Meanwhile, back in Nairobi, the Mitsubishi truck passes a bank and an office building on its way to the American Embassy's rear parking lot. Once it reaches the lot, it heads for the underground garage. When an embassy guard spots the truck approaching across the lot at high speed, he presses a button that drops a metal bar across the garage entrance.

A man in baggy pants and a plaid shirt jumps out of the truck's passenger side and demands that the guard raise the bar and let him through. The man hurls a grenade when the guard refuses. The guard ducks, and the grenade explodes somewhere behind him. Up above, in the windows of the embassy and the nearby bank and office building, faces appear behind the glass, looking curious and worried.

Back in Dar es Salaam, the Nissan truck remains thirty-five feet from the front gate, with the water tanker still blocking its way. It is 10:38 A.M. Five embassy guards are on duty at the gate. Two stand inside a guard booth and two stand behind it while the fifth guard stands near the water tanker.

At 10:39 A.M., the water tanker literally leaves Earth. The driver of the Nissan truck, a suicide bomber, has detonated the explosives inside his truck, and the force of the explosion has hurled the water tanker thirty feet into the air. The five embassy guards and the suicide bomber are dead before the tanker comes back to Earth. They are killed instantly

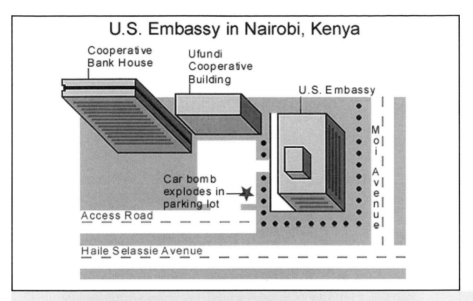

U.S. Embassy in Nairobi, Kenya

Cooperative Bank House

Ufundi Cooperative Building

U.S. Embassy

Moi Avenue

Car bomb explodes in parking lot

Access Road

Haile Selassie Avenue

The Ufundi Building, nearest the embassy in Nairobi, collapsed. Hundreds of people were buried under the rubble. Windows were shattered in the neighboring Cooperative Bank House.

by a force so powerful that the entire back wall of the embassy is peeled away, leaving staircases hanging in midair. If the water tanker, standing between the truck and the embassy, had not absorbed some of the force, the destruction would have been much worse.

At nearly the same instant in Nairobi, the other suicide bomber detonates his explosives, and the Mitsubishi truck in the rear parking lot is blown to bits. The destruction is far worse than in Dar es Salaam. Windows shatter in buildings all around, and people are struck with exploding glass. Many are killed instantly. The building nearest the embassy collapses, burying hundreds.

The final toll from the two blasts, which took place on August 7, 1998, was 224 killed and more than 5,000 injured. Twelve of the dead were Americans; most of the rest were African citizens.[1] None of these victims knew their attackers. They were victims of terrorism.

Terrorists Are Murderers

The U.S. Federal Bureau of Investigation (FBI) defines terrorism as ". . . the unlawful use of force or violence against persons or property to intimidate or coerce a government, the civilian population, or any segment thereof, in furtherance of political or social objectives."[2]

Terrorists' reasoning typically goes this way: They believe that their violence is justified because they commit it in the name of a political or social objective—a cause. Since this cause is a good one, they reason, they may use any means to achieve it, including violence.

But terrorism is not a legitimate means of achieving a cause, no matter how righteous, says Michael Sheehan, the U.S. State Department's coordinator for counterterrorism. "Terrorism is a crime, plain and simple," Sheehan says. "The fact that they [terrorists] espouse [adopt] a political or religious rhetoric does not change the fact that murder is murder."[3]

Terrorists Work for a Cause

Terrorists are not ordinary murderers, though. They work in their own special ways for their own special reasons. Whether they work alone or in groups, terrorists are true believers, dedicating their lives to a cause that they believe in completely.

Terrorist causes fall into three categories: political, ethnic, and religious. Political terrorists commit their crimes in the name of a political ideology, a set of ideas about how they believe society ought to operate. These terrorists oppose a nation's government because they think that government does not run things according to their beliefs. Some political terrorists are determined to replace the government with a new one that runs things their way. Other terrorists, known as anarchists, want to destroy the government and leave nothing in its place.

Ethnic terrorists commit their crimes in the name of a racial or cultural group, such as the Irish Catholics in Northern Ireland and the Tamils in Sri Lanka. These terrorists believe that a nation's government is oppressing them and treating them unfairly. They dedicate themselves to breaking away from this government and creating their own nation.

Religious terrorists believe that their criminal actions are justified by religious laws that are higher than any earthly laws. The embassy bombers were religious terrorists. They have been identified as extremist Muslims. Muslims are followers of the prophet Mohammed, and most Muslims are peaceful and law-abiding people. But extremist Muslims, like extremists of other faiths, sometimes carry their religious beliefs to violent extremes. They believe that killing those they perceive to be the enemies of God through acts of terrorism is a way to paradise in the next life. This may explain why the embassy bombers who drove the trucks were willing to be blown up with their bombs.

The men arrested for plotting the embassy bombings have been linked to al Qaeda, a Muslim terrorist organization. Al Qaeda is headed by Saudi multimillionaire Osama bin Laden, who calls himself a servant of Allah, the Arabic word for God. Bin Laden has been identified as the mastermind behind the bombings.

Bin Laden's primary enemy is not the United States, but Israel. In 1948, when the nation of Israel was created, Jews were given control of land that had once been controlled by the Muslims of Palestine. Muslims and Jews have fought over this land ever since. By supporting Israel, the United States has become an enemy of God in the opinion of extremists such as bin Laden and a prime target for Muslim terrorist groups like al Qaeda.

Terrorists Work in Secret

Terrorists must operate in secret because they are criminals and because they depend on the element of surprise to do their damage. Some terrorists, known as "lone wolves," work alone, but most terrorists work in small groups of ten or less. Small groups help to maintain secrecy. The smaller the group, the easier it will be for terrorists to keep their hiding places, membership, and activities secret.

These small groups are sometimes part of a larger organization. Even then, each small group's identity

Israel, now threatened by terrorists, became a Jewish state in part due to the actions of Zionist terrorists who were fighting for independence from the British.

is kept secret from the other groups, with each group operating independently in units called cells. This way, if terrorists from one cell should be captured, they will not be able to reveal very much about the other parts of the organization.

Terrorists are not soldiers or freedom fighters. Terrorists do not wear uniforms that identify them as members of a fighting force engaged in battle with another fighting force, as soldiers do. Terrorists do not fight small-scale actions against civil and military forces, as freedom fighters do. Terrorists operate in secret and in disguise, using hit-and-run tactics, like the embassy bombers, who struck suddenly and without warning, then vanished.

Terrorists Target Symbols of Authority

Terrorists target buildings, such as American embassies, that symbolize the nations and institutions they oppose. Other typical terrorist targets include churches and synagogues, police stations, army barracks, universities, corporate offices, banks, and various government buildings. Both the White House and the Pentagon, in Washington, D.C., have been terrorist targets. The embassy buildings in Africa symbolize the United States government that Osama bin Laden condemns as "unjust, criminal and tyrannical" for continuing to support Israel.[4]

Terrorists target people in positions of authority. These targets include elected officials, diplomats, judges, soldiers, police officers, business executives, news reporters, and university professors. Most of the time the terrorists have nothing personal against any of these people. Because they are part of the government, law enforcement, business, mass media, or education communities, they symbolize the society that the terrorists oppose.

Terrorists Kill Innocent People

Many terrorist victims were just at the wrong place at the wrong time. This is true of nearly all the embassy bombing victims. Only a few were in any way connected with the U.S. government. The rest were ordinary African citizens who happened to be nearby when the terrorist bombs exploded.

When innocent civilians are killed in a conventional war, both sides show regret. But to terrorists, there are no innocent civilians. Unlike soldiers or freedom fighters, terrorists do not recognize noncombatants. "We do not have to differentiate between military or civilian," says bin Laden. "As far as we are concerned, they are all targets."[5]

Terrorists Spread Fear

Terrorists seek to create change through fear. They use violence to make people so anxious and afraid that they will pressure their government to give in to terrorist demands. The 1998 embassy bombers did not have the numbers or the firepower to wage an open war against the military forces of Israel or America. Instead, these terrorists tried to create so much fear and anxiety that the U.S. government would drop its support for Israel.

To create this widespread atmosphere of fear, terrorists use murder, kidnapping, hostage-taking, hijacking, arson, and bombing. Now that explosives have become more compact and powerful, bombing has become the terrorist's weapon of choice.

For bombing targets, terrorists choose public places where people gather in numbers and expect to feel safe and secure. The U.S. embassies in Dar es Salaam and Nairobi were located in the midst of busy city centers in peaceful nations. By turning an ordinary morning in two secure public places into an explosive catastrophe, these terrorists sent an unspoken message: Look at what we can do. Look at the death and destruction we can spread. Your government cannot stop us. This could happen again at any time, any place, to any one of you—unless you give in to our demands.

Terrorists Use the News Media

Terrorism has been compared to theater. The public is the audience and the terrorists are the actors, trying to shock and frighten their audience. In order to reach the largest audience possible, they use the news media. A spectacular disaster, such as the embassy bombings, or a tense drama played out over days, weeks, or months, such as an airplane hijacking or a hostage-taking situation, is sure to be covered in the media. The more spectacular or tense the incident, the more news coverage it receives. This news coverage gives the terrorists what they want: the chance to frighten people and get their message across.

Terrorists Have Limited Success

Although the 1998 embassy bombers did not succeed in forcing America to change its policy toward Israel, some terrorist groups have achieved limited success, such as exchanging hostages for ransom or for the release of fellow terrorists from jails.

Other terrorist groups have succeeded in causing significant temporary damage to the governments they oppose. For example, by gunning down fifty-eight tourists in Luxor, Egypt, in 1996, a small group of terrorists succeeded in causing an estimated billion dollars' worth of damage to Egypt's tourist industry.[6]

Still other groups using terrorism have played a part in bringing about lasting change as part of a larger political movement. For example, during the 1930s and 1940s, a Hebrew military organization known as the Irgun Zvai Leumi (I.Z.L.) committed acts of terrorism and assassination in the Middle East. On April 9, 1947, Irgun commandos killed all 254 inhabitants of the Arab village of Dayr Yasin. This and other terrorist acts committed by the I.Z.L. contributed to the founding of the nation of Israel in 1948. Another group using terrorist tactics, the Irish Republican Army (IRA), played a part in securing independence for most of Northern Ireland from the British in 1922.

Despite these successes, very few terrorist groups ever see their ultimate goals accomplished. But lack of success has never stopped these groups from springing up again and again throughout history.

2

Terrorism Involving Americans

Terrorist groups began appearing in America during the mid–1800s. During this time emigrants were flocking to America from Europe in search of a better life. Most of these new arrivals had to take low-paying factory and mining jobs with long hours, harsh working conditions, and no labor unions. At this time in American history, workers had little in the way of power to demand better conditions. When these conditions became too harsh, some workers turned to terrorism because they felt it was the only way to change things.

The Molly Maguires

One of these early terrorist groups sprang up among Irish immigrant coal miners in eastern Pennsylvania in the 1860s. When management refused to listen to their demands for better pay and relief from harsh working conditions in the mines, they turned to terrorism. The group took the name of a legendary Irish heroine who was supposed to have led a peasant revolt. They called themselves the Molly Maguires.

The Molly Maguires used violence, including murder, to terrorize wealthy mine owners and their bosses as well as the police who protected them. A private detective managed to infiltrate the group and expose its terrorist activities. The group failed to

Some mine bosses received what the Molly Maguires called a "coffin notice." This was meant as a warning of what would happen if they failed to meet the group's demands.

bring about positive changes to miners' working conditions, and it dissolved in 1877, when ten or twenty (reports conflict) of the Molly Maguires were convicted of murder and put to death.

The KKK

The largest and deadliest terrorist group in America also sprang up around this same time, but for different reasons. It was known as the Ku Klux Klan (KKK). Ku Klux comes from the Greek word for "circle," and Klan is another way of spelling clan, which means "a group of related families." The KKK took root as a result of racial problems.

When the American Civil War ended in 1865, a tumultuous period in American history known as Reconstruction began. Southern black men who had been slaves before the Civil War were suddenly citizens with the same constitutional rights as the Southern white men who used to be their masters. Black men could now vote, hold elected office, and own land.

Some of these Southern white men could not accept this new state of affairs. They were white supremacists. They believed that the white race was superior to all other races. One December night in 1865 in the little town of Pulaski, Tennessee, six of these angry white men draped themselves in white sheets, jumped on their horses, and went galloping through the black community, whooping and hollering that they had "come up from hell."[1]

When they saw how their nighttime ride had shaken the black men and women of the town, they continued their terrorist rides, stirring up more fear and anxiety in the black community. The news of these terrorist rides spread, and KKK groups sprang up in one Southern state after another, with deadly violence following in their wake. White Klansmen beat, whipped, mutilated, shot, and hung their black victims.

An alarmed federal government responded by passing a series of anti-Klan laws and sending in federal troops to enforce them. The results were swift and sure. Membership in Klan groups dropped off, and

The Ku Klux Klan came into existence in 1865, after black Americans were freed from slavery. Members of the Ku Klux Klan, which still exists, are white supremacists who engaged in terrorist acts against people their members believe to be inferior.

by 1871 these white supremacist terrorist groups were nearly dead.

But the KKK was reborn in 1915 as tens of thousands of immigrants came to America from Europe. The reborn Klan had new targets on whom to focus their racial hatred. Now they targeted anyone who was not a white Protestant, especially newly arrived Catholics and Jews. Klansmen blamed their targets for rising unemployment and crime rates. There were more terrorist beatings, whippings, shootings, and hangings, with the reborn Klan active in the Midwest as well as the South. By the mid-1920s, Klan membership had swelled to an estimated 4 million.[2] But once again the government responded with new anti-Klan laws, and once again Klan membership dropped—for the time being.

The IRA

At the same time, in the early 1920s, in Ireland, terrorism was on the rise. This terrorism and the conditions that caused it were of concern to many of the Americans whose immediate ancestors had come to America from Ireland.

The roots of terrorism in Ireland reach back to the twelfth century when Britain gained control of Ireland. Since then, the Irish have rebelled against the ruling British time and again, and each time the more powerful British have struck back, crushing one Irish rebellion after another. Religious differences between the two ethnic groups have continually fueled the conflict, with the majority of the British being Protestant and the majority of the Irish being Catholic.

From these centuries of conflict, a terrorist group of Irish Catholics known as the Irish Republican Army (IRA) was born. The IRA's goal was to eliminate all British control and make Ireland a free and independent nation. The IRA was opposed by Irish Protestants as well as by the British. The guns and explosives used in IRA terrorist attacks came from money supplied by sympathizers in both Ireland and the United States. In 1922, Britain granted independence to most of Ireland. Pressure from the terrorist activities of the IRA helped convince the British to let go.

But the British did not let go of Ireland entirely. Six counties in the north, a region known as Ulster, where Protestants were in the majority, remained under British rule. The IRA, however, would settle for nothing less than a totally free, independent, and united Ireland, and they vowed to fight the British until Ulster, too, was independent.

At first the IRA confined their terrorist attacks to British policemen and soldiers. But by the 1960s they had extended their targets to British civilians, setting off bombs in public places in Ulster and in Britain itself.

IRA terrorists continued their battle all through the rest of the twentieth century and are still fighting in the twenty-first. Americans continue to support the IRA. Between 1995 and 2000, Americans donated $3.5 million to the IRA cause, on the condition that it be used by Sinn Fein, the political wing of the IRA, for negotiating a peaceful settlement and not for the purchase of guns.[3] Despite repeated attempts at making peace, the British and Irish continue their dispute, and the IRA continues its terrorist attacks.

The KKK Returns

The Ku Klux Klan was reborn once again in the United States in the 1960s. This rebirth came when Congress passed the Civil Rights Act of 1964. This legislation was designed to put an end to racial segregation in the South, where black people were not allowed to attend schools and use public facilities, such as restaurants and bathrooms, reserved for whites. African Americans had to use separate, inferior facilities instead.

Angry Klan members responded with some of the same terrorist tactics the Klan had used during Reconstruction one hundred years earlier. KKK terrorists hoped to spread so much fear through the South that the federal government would stop trying to end segregation. But despite this deadly terrorism, schools and public facilities in the South were successfully integrated. The KKK failed in its terrorist mission, and Klan membership dropped once again.

The KKK still exists in the twenty-first century. In 1998 Klan members in Texas were arrested by agents of the FBI before they could carry out a plot to bomb a natural gas facility. In rallies in various states, Klan leaders continue to proclaim their hatred of African Americans, Jews, gays, lesbians, communists, the federal government, and the mass media. Today's

Klan consists of a few scattered groups without a central organization, and small numbers of Klan members continue to engage in terrorist activities and preach hate.

Counterculture Terrorists

The South was not the only region of America where terrorists struck during the 1960s. All over the nation, men and women who violently disagreed with certain policies of universities, big business, and the federal government took up arms against them and committed terrorist acts.

These terrorists fought in the name of a number of causes, which journalists lumped together under the term *counterculture*. Some counterculture terrorists fought against racism, committing terrorist acts in order to force the government to do more to end segregation. Others committed terrorist acts against universities that did research for the government and against banks and other business institutions that represented the capitalist economic system that they saw as oppressing the poor.

One cause that many counterculture terrorists fought for was ending the Vietnam War. Starting in the late 1960s, the federal government sent hundreds of thousands of American troops to the southeast Asian nation of Vietnam. Their mission was to aid government forces in South Vietnam in their fight with guerrilla forces, known as the Viet Cong, who were aided by North Vietnam.

Since the Viet Cong were given weapons and

money by the communist nations of Russia and China, supporters of American involvement saw the war as a battle against communism, a political system at odds with American democracy.

But many U.S. citizens thought America had no business getting involved in another nation's civil war halfway around the world. A small number of those citizens were so strongly opposed to the Vietnam War that they took up arms against their own government. They became antiwar terrorists within the United States, determined to force their government to bring U.S. troops home from Vietnam.

Most antiwar terrorists operated alone or in very small groups. The largest group, never more than a few hundred strong, was known as Weatherman. Nearly all were college-educated people in their twenties. Weathermen were responsible for armed robberies to finance their activities, as well as sniper attacks and bombings designed to terrorize the police and public.

Weatherman saw America's involvement in Vietnam as an attempt to dominate a smaller nation without actually taking direct control of its government, a tactic known as imperialism. Weatherman announced that its ultimate goal was nothing less than to "totally destroy this imperialist and racist society."[4]

Bombs were the weapon of choice for Weatherman as well as for other counterculture terrorist groups of the 1960s. Buildings from coast to coast belonging to universities, big business, the U.S. Army, and the federal, state, and city governments became prime targets for these terrorist bombers. Targets included university science and mathematics buildings, banks, a courthouse, a newspaper office, military induction centers, New York City police headquarters, a consulate building, the Pentagon, and the U.S. Capitol Building. Eugene T. Rossides, assistant secretary of the Treasury, stated that "from January 1969 to April of this year [1970]. . . this country suffered a total of 4,330 bombings, an additional 1,475 attempted bombings, and a reported 35,129 threatened bombings."[5]

Antiwar terrorist activity in the United States hit its peak in 1970. After that, it slowly declined as U.S. troops were steadily withdrawn from Vietnam. Troop withdrawals came partly as a result of the pressure brought on the federal government by the antiwar movement, which included these terrorist activities. With the Vietnam War's end in 1975, antiwar terrorism came to an end as well.

The FALN

In the 1970s and early 1980s, a new kind of terrorist group sprang up in America. This was the Puerto Rican nationalist group know as the FALN, which stands for *Fuerzas Armadas de Liberacion Nacional*, or Armed Forces of National Liberation.

The Caribbean island of Puerto Rico is a self-governing commonwealth under the protection of the United States. It is not a state, but it is not its own nation either. The FALN engaged in terrorist activities with the goal of securing that island's unconditional independence from the United States.

FBI officials accused the FALN of taking part in more than one hundred bombing incidents in cities across America. These bombings resulted in six deaths, eighty injuries, and over $3.5 million in property damage. In the Chicago area alone, between 1975 and 1980, FALN members were implicated in twenty-eight separate bombings.[6]

The FALN suffered a crippling blow in April 1980 when twelve of its members were arrested while plotting a kidnapping near Chicago, Illinois. All twelve FALN terrorists received prison terms ranging from a few months to thirty years.

With most of their leaders in jail, this terrorist group has been quiet since the early 1980s. But the FALN continues to exist. In a 1999 report issued by U.S. Attorney General Janet Reno, the group was referred to as an "ongoing threat" to national security.[7] In that same year, President Bill Clinton released sixteen FALN members who had been given long prison terms when they pledged not to engage in any violent activities.

Target: Americans Abroad

Throughout the 1970s and 1980s, Americans abroad were a prime terrorist target. Some targets were tourists on vacation. Others were diplomats, soldiers, university professors, and business executives serving their country, teaching, or working abroad.

Many Americans were targeted by Muslim terrorist groups in the Middle East, including Hamas and the Islamic Jihad. Like bin Laden's al Qaeda, these Muslim extremist terrorist groups violently objected to America's continuing support of Israel. They used shooting, bombing, airline hijacking, and hostage-taking as their primary weapons.

In the deadliest ground attack by Middle Eastern terrorist groups, a suicide bomber drove a truck full of dynamite into the U.S. Marine headquarters in Beirut, Lebanon, in October of 1983. Ethnic and religious factions in the Middle Eastern nation of Lebanon were fighting an ongoing civil war in which Israel and other states were deeply involved. The U.S. Marines were part of a multinational force attempting to promote peace in Lebanon. The Islamic Jihad staged the attack in order to drive these peacekeepers from their nation. The attack killed 241 Marines and sailors.[8]

The deadliest airline bombing by Muslim terrorists took place in December 1988 over Lockerbie, Scotland. A Pan Am jumbo jet en route to New York from Germany blew apart in midair. The bomb was in a suitcase, packed inside a Toshiba radio-cassette player. The two men held responsible for smuggling the suitcase onto the plane were believed to be Libyan spies posing as Libyan Arab Airlines employees. All 259 passengers and crew members died, along with eleven people on the ground. Among the Americans killed onboard the plane were thirty-five students from Syracuse University.[9]

Not all of these terrorist incidents focused on

America's support of Israel. The longest-running hostage crisis involving Americans abroad focused on America's interference with another nation's government. In 1952, combined U.S. and British secret service forces helped overthrow the Iranian prime minister, Mohammad Mossadeq, and replace him with Mohammad Reza Shah Pahlavi, known as the Shah.

The Shah of Iran remained friendly with the United States throughout the 1950s, 1960s, and 1970s. He used a brutal secret police force, the Savak, to help keep himself power. Finally, in February of 1979, the Shah's government was overthrown and replaced by a revolutionary government headed by fundamentalist Muslims. These revolutionaries feared that the United States would once again interfere with Iranian political affairs and attempt to return the Shah to power.

In this atmosphere of fear and distrust, some of these revolutionaries turned to terrorism. On November 4, 1979, a crowd of about 500 Iranians, most of them students, seized the American embassy in Tehran. Of the approximately 90 people inside, 52 were American embassy employees. The students took these Americans hostage. After a failed rescue attempt and months of negotiations, the hostages were finally freed in January 1981, 444 days after being taken captive.[10]

It is important to note here that terrorism is not confined to the Middle East. Terrorism occurs all around the world. Through the 1970s and 1980s, though, the most serious terrorism against Americans occurred in the Middle East. Since the 1980s, though, there have been fewer attacks on Americans abroad.

The World Trade Center Bombing

The decade of the 1990s was punctuated by three explosive terrorist attacks on American soil that each changed the way Americans look at their homeland. The attacks were not related. Each attack was carried out by a different terrorist or terrorist group.

The first of these attacks on American soil came on Friday, February 26, 1993, at the World Trade Center in New York City. The Trade Center consists of twin 110-story towers. More than 180,000 people come into the towers on a typical weekday. At 12:18 P.M., a rented truck parked in the garage beneath the twin towers exploded, smashing through the building's foundation. Six people were killed and more than a thousand were wounded. Damage was in the tens of millions of dollars.[11]

The four terrorists who were convicted of the bombing were militant Muslims from the Middle East. They sought revenge for United States involvement in Middle Eastern political affairs. They succeeded in shocking the nation. Nothing like this had ever happened on American soil before. New York Governor Mario Cuomo said, "No foreign people or force has ever done this to us. Until now, we were invulnerable."[12]

The Oklahoma City Bombing

The second terrorist attack within U.S. borders took place in Oklahoma City, Oklahoma, on April 19,

1995. The target was the Alfred P. Murrah Federal Building.

The nine stories of the Murrah Building are home to twenty-two separate government offices, including offices of the U.S. Army and Marine Corps, the Department of Defense, the U.S. Secret Service, and the Bureau of Alcohol, Tobacco and Firearms (ATF). The Murrah Building could present a tempting target for someone who feared and hated the federal government.

Timothy McVeigh believed that his government had turned against the American people. He believed it was plotting to take away everyone's basic freedoms. He rented a truck and loaded it with a bomb made from fertilizer and fuel oil. McVeigh armed the 4,800-pound bomb with a timing device and parked the truck in front of the Murrah Federal Building.

McVeigh was on his way out of town at 9:08 A.M. when the bomb exploded. The blast sank a crater eight feet deep and twenty feet in diameter into the earth. A total of 168 people were killed and more than five hundred were injured.[13]

McVeigh was caught, tried, and found guilty, and sentenced to death on June 13, 1997. McVeigh was executed on June 11, 2001. An accomplice who had helped McVeigh plan the bombing, Terry Nichols, was sentenced to life in prison in 1998. McVeigh's ultimate goal was to cause a general rebellion against the federal government. Instead of rebellion, he caused fear and anxiety throughout the United States. As news analyst Joe Klein wrote, the Oklahoma City bombing had made a significant contribution to "the growing sense that our most basic assumptions of security, of rationality, of decency are more tenuous than we had ever imagined."[14]

The Unabomber

The third explosive terrorist attack on American soil was actually a series of attacks, sixteen in all, stretching over an eighteen-year period from 1978 to 1996. Sixteen times an innocent person opened what appeared to be an ordinary letter or package, and sixteen times the letter or package exploded.

These mail bombs killed three people and injured twenty-three. Some victims were university professors. Others were business executives with computer companies, lumber companies, and airlines.

All these attacks were the work of the same elusive individual. The FBI gave this unknown terrorist the name Unabomber because the early targets of his mailbombs were people connected with *UN*iversities and *A*irlines. The Unabomber was finally arrested in April 1996 in a cabin in the remote Montana wilderness. His name was Ted Kaczynski. On May 4, 1998, Kaczynski was sentenced to life in prison.

What kind of person was Ted Kaczynski? What would make a man devote sixteen years of his life to constructing bombs aimed at people he had never met? What kind of person was Timothy McVeigh? What would drive a man to kill and injure hundreds of innocent strangers? Who is Osama bin Laden? Why has he dedicated his life to terrorism?

If we could somehow look into the mind of a terrorist, what would we see?

3

How Terrorists See the World

Most modern terrorists are young males, but there are exceptions. There are female and middle-aged terrorists. And each of these people, male or female, young or old, is a unique person. But there are a few things that can be said about terrorists and how they see the world, based on their actions and what they have said and written.

Terrorists Are Extremists

For one thing, terrorists are extremists. They take their beliefs to the limit. Extremists are absolutely certain that everything they

32

believe is correct. They are unreasonable as well as uncompromising. When the embassy bombers set off their truckloads of explosives, they were not trying to change people's minds through any sort of reasonable, rational appeal. They were trying to eliminate opposition by blasting it away, and they did not care who got injured or killed in the process.

Terrorists Are Intolerant

". . . what is dangerous about extremists is not that they are extreme," wrote Attorney General Robert F. Kennedy, "but that they are intolerant. The evil is not what they say about their cause, but what they say about their opponents."[1]

Terrorists often refer to their enemies as less than human—as animals. Here is how one terrorist leader, Ulrike Meinhof, referred to the policemen that she and her group had targeted for death: "We say the guy in uniform is a pig, not a human being, and we have to tackle him from this point of view."[2] Meinhof led a small gang of urban terrorists in West Germany who robbed banks and bombed buildings in the early 1970s. They were loosely connected with counterculture student radicals in America.

By dehumanizing their opponents in this way, by showing them absolutely no respect, terrorists can feel free to do anything they want to them, including murder. For this same reason, terrorists often refer to their opponents as devilish monsters. The Iranian terrorists who held the fifty-two American hostages prisoner for 444 days referred to the United States as "the Great Satan." Calling their opponents children of Satan makes them that much easier to kidnap and kill.

Terrorists Are Power Hungry

Terrorists see the world as a battleground. Every day is another day of combating the enemy. In the terrorist's eyes, people are naturally mean to one another, and they treat each other cruelly because that is the nature of humankind. In this savage sort of world, it makes no sense to deal fairly with others and keep promises and respect laws that the majority of people share.

In the terrorists' world, the only rules to follow and the only laws to obey are their own. This kind of thinking gives them a sense of power, which they crave. While other people look for approval, terrorists look for fear. Making people fear them helps make them feel powerful and in control.

Terrorists Are Idealistic

To terrorists, the world is an unjust place where the evil rule the good while the rich and powerful oppress the poor and powerless. They long for a brand-new world where things work according to their ideals, where the people who are good in their eyes are rewarded and the evil are punished. And they are willing to dedicate their lives to making this brand new world a reality. To make this happen, terrorists believe they must first destroy the existing world and sweep it aside to make room for this new, better world, where things work according to their beliefs.

Terrorists Seek Revenge

Terrorists are destructive because they feel that violence is their only choice, that nothing else can change the world. And even when terrorists see that their violence is not getting them anywhere, they continue, because whether it works or not, violence does get them something.

Terrorists use violence to get revenge. Even if they cannot truly change the world, they can at least cause pain and fear. Terrorists are obsessed with dealing out punishment to their enemies. If they cannot defeat them, they can at least punish them. Some terrorism experts believe that causing fear and pain is the terrorist's real goal. Stephen Carter, a Yale University law school professor, writes: "If terrorists can cause us to become a closed and fearful society, they win. And that's their point."[3]

Case Study: Timothy McVeigh

What was Timothy McVeigh's goal? What drove him to construct a 4,800-pound bomb and set it off in front of the Murrah Federal Building, killing 168 people, including nineteen children, and injuring more than five hundred others?[4] What was going on in this terrorist's mind?

McVeigh joined the U.S. Army in 1988, when he was twenty. He was a young man with a dream. He would dedicate himself to becoming a Green Beret, a member of an elite Special Forces fighting unit, and fight glorious battles that would make his friends and family proud of him.

In 1991 McVeigh's army infantry unit was sent to Iraq to fight in the Gulf War. After the war, McVeigh qualified to join an intensive training program for the elite Special Forces unit he dreamed of joining. But after just two days of training, McVeigh's dream died. He dropped out of the Special Forces program. The training was too much for him. "I am not physically ready," he wrote.[5]

Back in the regular army now, McVeigh had to live with his disappointment. He did not live with it well. One soldier who knew him then said that McVeigh was angry and upset most of the time, full of frustrations and complaints.

McVeigh directed his complaints at the federal government as well as the army, especially the FBI and the Bureau of Alcohol, Tobacco and Firearms (ATF). These federal law enforcement agencies had become too powerful, he insisted. McVeigh was convinced that government leaders were using these agencies to take away citizens' most cherished freedoms, including the right to bear arms as guaranteed in the Second Amendment to the Constitution.

McVeigh began building up an arsenal, ordering weapons from catalogs and buying them at gun shows. His collection included a machine gun, pistols, shotguns, and rifles. McVeigh kept them in the trunk of his car, and he began carrying a 9 mm Glock pistol with him wherever he went.

McVeigh also carried a copy of a novel, *The*

Turner Diaries, which he would urge people to read. In this fictional tale by William Pierce, the federal government does exactly what McVeigh feared it would do. It takes guns away from people and throws anyone who objects into prison.

The evil individuals who run this corrupt government in Pierce's fictional tale are Jews and African Americans, while the people who oppose them are white supremacists who call themselves patriots. The goal of these white supremacists is to rally citizens all over the United States to rise up in violent revolution and overthrow the corrupt federal government.

The supremacists intend to accomplish this goal by bombing government buildings. In *The Turner Diaries*, members of this terrorist group build a bomb from fertilizer and rocket fuel, load it onto a truck, park it in front of a federal building at nine in the morning, and detonate it, causing massive loss of life. Later, on April 19, 1995, in Oklahoma City, Oklahoma, McVeigh would turn Pierce's vicious fictional attack into a real-life catastrophe.

With his fear and hatred of the federal government, McVeigh was now extremely uncomfortable as a soldier in his nation's armed forces. In his eyes, the government he had been trained to fight for would soon be waging an all-out war against its own people. If McVeigh had to fight in that war, it would be against his government, not for it. So in December of 1991, McVeigh left the Army.

Back in western New York state, where he had grown up, McVeigh wrote angry letters to newspapers. "AMERICA IS IN SERIOUS DECLINE," he wrote in

A crane picks up wreckage from the destruction caused by Timothy McVeigh's terrorist bomb.

capital letters. "Do we have to shed blood to reform the current system? I hope it doesn't come to that. But it might."[6]

Because his views were so extreme and violent, McVeigh found himself spending more and more time with people who had the same view of the world as he had. Some of these people belonged to white supremacist hate groups, such as the KKK. Others belonged to paramilitary groups, also known as militias. Militia members arm themselves heavily and engage in training exercises to prepare themselves to do battle with the federal government.

McVeigh was particularly outraged over a battle that federal agents had fought in April 1993 with a religious cult near Waco, Texas. This cult, known as the Branch Davidians, had amassed a stockpile of weapons. Many of these weapons were illegal, but the cult would not give them up to federal agents. Each side blamed the other for starting the gun battle, which led to the cult's buildings being burnt to the ground. About eighty cult members died in the fire. Twenty-five of them were children. McVeigh saw the Waco battle as proof that all his worst fears about the federal government and the FBI were coming true.

Two years later, McVeigh took action against the federal government. When he was planning the bombing, McVeigh told a friend he had met in the army, Michael Fortier, that he would have to get a lot of attention, which meant that he would have to kill a great many people. Fortier was later sentenced to prison for his failure to inform anyone of McVeigh's plans. "He told me that he was wanting to blow up a building to cause a general uprising in America," Fortier said, "and hopefully that would knock some people off the fence and urge them into taking action against the federal government."[7]

McVeigh set out to kill as many people as he could with the intent of spearheading a revolution that would overthrow the entire U.S. government. Like other terrorists, McVeigh was an extremist. He was intolerant of anyone who did not agree with him. He was alienated from the world around him and hungry for the power to change it. He wanted to remake the world the way he thought it ought to be. However, he was unrealistic in thinking that he could achieve this goal by setting off a bomb that killed and injured hundreds of innocent people.

4

How Terrorists Operate

In addition to food, clothing, and shelter, terrorists need cash to buy the weapons, vehicles, and other equipment for their violent work. But normal, day-to-day sources of income (steady jobs) are not open to them. Their secretive, nomadic lifestyle will not allow them to stay in one place for long.

Money was not a problem for Timothy McVeigh. He was not a full-time terrorist or part of a terrorist group. His terrorism consisted of a single act. McVeigh was able to buy the fertilizer, rocket fuel, and oil drums and rent the truck to carry the bomb with a few thousand dollars of his own.

41

But what about full-time terrorists? How do they get the steady flow of money they must have to live and operate?

Financing Their Operations

Some full-time terrorists rob banks and armored cars. Robbery was a major source of income for the members of Weatherman and other counterculture groups of the 1960s. The IRA also uses robberies to help finance its terrorist operations. Some modern terrorists, especially groups in Central and South America, finance their operations through selling drugs.

Ransoms obtained from kidnappings is another source of income. Terrorist kidnappings of Americans jumped dramatically in the 1990s along with a surge in American tourism overseas, especially in South America. Most, but not all, of these kidnappings end with the hostages being returned safely after a ransom is paid.

Not all terrorist money comes through violence. Some of it comes from contributions. Some people believe so strongly in the cause of a terrorist group that they donate money or weapons. Between 1995 and 1999, for instance, Americans contributed an estimated $3.5 million to the IRA.[1]

National governments also contribute to terrorism. This practice is known as state-sponsored terrorism. Libya, Iraq, Syria, Iran, Sudan, Cuba, and North Korea have been identified as state sponsors of terrorism by the U.S. State Department. Pakistan and Afghanistan, while not on the list, have been criticized for giving terrorists places to live. These nations, with the exception of Cuba and North Korea, supply cash, weapons, and homes for Muslim terrorist groups such as Hamas and Hizbollah. These nations and terrorist groups share a common hatred of Israel and the United States.

Osama bin Laden's terrorist network, al Qaeda, has a unique way of getting its money. Much of it comes from a single source—bin Laden himself. He is credited with raising some of the millions of dollars needed to operate al Qaeda from nations that sponsor Muslim terrorists. Bin Laden himself is credited with contributing the rest from his own vast fortune. His late father accumulated hundreds of millions of dollars from a construction empire he created in Saudi Arabia. Bin Laden inherited an estimated quarter of a billion dollars when his father died.

In 1979, at the age of twenty-two, bin Laden left Saudi Arabia to fight in Afghanistan. Russian troops had invaded that Muslim nation. With his inherited fortune, bin Laden helped fund the Afghan resistance fighters, the Mujahedeen, who won their war against Russian troops in 1989. In return for his help fighting the Russians, Afghanistan has been giving Osama bin Laden and his al Qaeda terrorist network a home base from which to operate ever since.

Planning Their Attacks

Since their secret operations depend on precise timing, terrorists must put careful thought into planning their attacks. First, they carefully observe their target. If the target is a person to be kidnapped or taken hostage, the terrorists study their target's habits and movements during a typical day and plan their attack around their target's daily schedule.

Through careful planning and skillful execution, a few terrorists can do the work of a small army. Twenty members of one terrorist group managed to take more than five hundred people hostage at the residence of the Japanese ambassador to Peru by attacking during a party in December 1996.[2] Members of the group, known as the Tupac Amaru Revolutionary Movement (MRTA), used explosives to break through a security wall. As they broke in, other members of the group who had gotten into the party disguised as waiters and caterers were already there, waiting to help them. In April 1997, police and military units stormed the embassy, killing all the terrorists and releasing all but one of the hostages.

If the target is a public building to be bombed, the terrorists study the building's layout to decide where to place the bomb so it will do the most damage. They also study the building's security system and traffic patterns in order to know where and when to detonate the bomb to hurt the most people without getting caught.

The men who planned the World Trade Center bombing chose an underground parking garage in order to direct the explosive force of the blast upward through the center of the entire structure. According to a State Department counterterrorism expert, it would have taken a bomb ten times bigger to do as much damage outside the building.[3] The bombers had hoped the blast would shake the structure's foundation enough to topple one tower into another. Fortunately, the towers remained standing and six people were killed instead of the tens of thousands the terrorists had hoped for.[4]

Terrorists must get hold of the weapons they need. In the case of bombs, they build their weapons themselves. Both Timothy McVeigh and the World Trade Center bombers built their bombs from materials that are available to anyone who wants to buy them. Plans on how to build bombs of all kinds are also available. "People who feel that the bomb might be their weapon of choice now have the information to make one," said Al Gleason, a retired federal agent.[5]

Striking Their Targets

Terrorist attacks are surprise attacks. Terrorists hit and run. They have to, since terrorism is a matter of the weak (the terrorists) attacking the strong (the established order of society). The terrorist message is clear: We will strike, but you will never know where, when, or who. It could be any of you, any place, any time.

Terrorist tactics traditionally include assassinations and murders, kidnapping, bombing, and skyjacking (airline hijacking). During the 1970s and 1980s there were a great number of skyjackings. Many were staged by Muslim terrorist organizations, such as the Popular Front for the Liberation of Palestine (PFLP). The skyjackers would manage to smuggle weapons aboard a commercial airliner, then hold the plane, crew, and passengers hostage.

The skyjackers would then make their demands, which usually included a ransom that might run into the millions of dollars, the release of fellow terrorists from prisons, and safe passage for the skyjackers.

Skyjackers seldom get what they ask for, and sometimes end up dead. In 1976, five PFLP members, along with two West German terrorists, skyjacked an Air France Airbus heading from Israel to France. Most of the passengers were Israeli citizens. The terrorists ordered the pilot to fly to Entebbe, Uganda, in east Africa, because the skyjackers had the cooperation of Ugandan dictator Idi Amin. Their plans went awry when Israeli commandos flew to Uganda and struck back, storming the plane, killing the terrorists, and rescuing the passengers.

Terrorists sometimes strike airliners with bombs. They manage to smuggle explosives on board that eventually are detonated by a timing device while the plane is in midair. In 1988, Pan Am Flight 103, on its way from Frankfurt, Germany, to New York with 259 passengers on board, was blown up over Lockerbie, Scotland. Plastic explosives such as RDX or Semtex probably were used.[6] These explosives can pack tremendous power into a small package and cannot be detected by airport metal detectors. There were no survivors, making it one of the worst terrorist attacks on record.

The Weapon of Choice

Terrorists use bombing more than any other method of attack. According to the U.S. Department of State, of the 111 terrorist attacks against Americans in 1998, 96 were by bombing.[7] Terrorists favor bombing for several reasons. Bombs can be hidden away and smuggled to their target in a variety of ways. The Pan Am 103 bomb was concealed in a radio-cassette player. And bombs can do their work at a safe distance from the terrorists who plant them. Even the large, cumbersome bombs used by Timothy McVeigh and the World Trade Center bombers did not hurt their makers, who used timing devices to detonate them once they had gotten safely out of range.

Terrorists have used deadly ingenuity in delivering bombs to their targets. On October 12, 2000, two terrorists delivered their bomb by sea. Their target was the U.S.S. *Cole*. The U.S. Navy warship was in the process of refueling in the port of Aden, the capital city of Yemen, a country in southwest Arabia. At 11:18 A.M., the two suicide bombers drove their small boat, a motorized skiff, directly into the side of the warship, tearing a 40–by–40 foot hole in its side. Early reports from investigators indicated that the powerful plastic explosive C–4 was used.

Potential suspects included members of several Middle Eastern terrorist groups. Investigators named Osama bin Laden as the likely mastermind behind the attack, which left seventeen U.S. sailors dead and thirty-nine more wounded.[8]

The fear factor is another reason terrorists favor bombs. Bombs have enormous shock value. They make a lot of noise, and their destructiveness is purely random. Anyone within range could be hurt or killed. Bombs are seen and heard a good distance away in all directions from the blast itself: The embassy bomb in Nairobi shattered windows a quarter of a mile away. And bombs result in widespread

The 40-foot-by-40-foot hole torn in the U.S.S. Cole's side by suicide bombers.

property damage as well as loss of life and property. Buildings collapse. Smoke rises high in the sky, to be seen for miles around. Police vehicles and fire trucks and ambulances rush to the scene from all directions, along with television camera crews and news reporters coming to document this dramatic scene of horror the terrorists have created for all the world to see.

If the attack is a bombing, the terrorists flee, leaving their victims behind. Later, they may phone police, a newspaper office, or a television or radio station to claim responsibility, make demands, and threaten to strike again if their demands are not met. If no one claims responsibility and no demands are made, the attack becomes a mystery for the media and police to unravel, like the Unabomber mail bombings.

Getting Publicity

Terrorists of all kinds use the news media to get publicity for their causes and to help spread fear and anxiety. Terrorists want the media to portray them in a sympathetic light. They try to be seen as the underdog,

A sailor who survived the bombing of the U.S.S. Cole *is comforted on arrival home.*

as brave little Davids fighting mean, lumbering Goliaths. They want to be seen as concerned human beings fighting cruel forces far more powerful than themselves in the name of a noble cause. They want the public to see their criminal violence as a last resort, a tactic they are using only because they have no other way to achieve their goals. And terrorists want the media to portray them in an attractive light. Instead of being seen as common criminals, they want to be portrayed as mysterious, daring, coura-geous, and free spirited.

Use of the media by terrorists has been called a form of political advertising and public relations. Some terrorist groups actually do have members who are assigned to deal with the media, acting as spokespersons for the group. Sinn Fein is the most sophisticated example. This political wing of the IRA, a legal political party, works directly with the news media, holding press conferences, issuing demands, negotiating with the ruling government, and giving interviews on the group's behalf.

The news media may not always portray terrorists as they would like to be seen, but they do cover terrorist attacks. Terrorism is always big news because it is so violent and frightening. And in the case of television news, terrorism makes an ideal subject because it is so visual: mysterious masked men waving automatic weapons, bombs making great clouds of smoke and walls of fire, collapsed buildings, rescuers digging for trapped survivors, tearful survivors telling their tales of near death. This is news that people will watch, so it is news that television will continue to broadcast even though it means giving terrorists the publicity they crave.

The Debate Over Media Coverage

Some people think the news media should use more restraint in covering terrorist stories. They argue that coverage encourages terrorism by giving terrorists what they cannot get any other way: a worldwide stage on which to announce their message. British news analyst John O'Sullivan says that "if the media were not there to report terrorist acts and to explain their political and social significance (the motives inspiring them and so forth), terrorism as such would cease to exist."[9]

In a closed society, such as North Korea or Libya, the ruling government can stop the media from reporting news that it does not want the public to know about, including news of terrorist attacks. But in a free and open society, such as the United States, the government could not do this. Banning news coverage of a terrorist incident would be a clear violation of the First Amendment right of free speech. Terrorists have sometimes used this freedom to manipulate the news media.

Case Study: The Iran Hostage Crisis

Critics of unrestrained media coverage of terrorism point to the Iran hostage drama as a clear example of terrorists manipulating the news media. Iranian terrorists took Americans hostage to pay the United States back for its support of an Iranian dictator. For decades the United States had supported the Shah of Iran, a dictator who helped introduce liberal Western customs and morals into Iran's deeply conservative Muslim culture. Western books, movies, television, clothing, food, and drink had come to Tehran and other big cities in Iran during the Shah's reign.

Many Iranians were deeply offended by Western sexual freedom and the freedoms women enjoyed in education and the workplace. When the hostages were taken, Iran was in the midst of a revolution meant to turn back this invasion of Western ways. The Shah had been thrown out and a conservative Muslim leader, the Ayatollah Khomeni, now ruled in his place. Traditional Muslim ways were back in force now, and Western ways were outlawed.

The Iranian terrorists held the hostages and staged their demonstrations to get revenge for America's support of the Shah and to show the American people that things were different in Iran now. During the 444 days that the 52 American hostages were held in the American Embassy in Tehran, terrorists staged numerous demonstrations for the American television cameras. They brought the blindfolded hostages outside and paraded them before the news cameras while shouting anti-American slogans, waving anti-American signs, and burning the American flag.

All of this was broadcast into American living rooms on the nightly news for the entire 444 days that the hostages were held. Would the hostage situation have gone on for so long if the American news media had not kept giving the terrorists what they wanted? Here is the view of political commentator Charles Krauthammer:

> The American hostages would not have been held so long had the Iranians not realized that they had created the most effective television stage in history, which gave them immediate access to millions of people. The Iranians exploited the hostage crisis in a way that they could not have done in the absence of television cameras.[10]

Case Study: The Unabomber Manifesto

Some people favor unrestrained media coverage of terrorist events. These people point to the case of the Unabomber. In this case, the news media gave the terrorist the publicity he demanded, and this publicity led directly to his downfall.

For eighteen years, the Unabomber killed and maimed people with mail bombs. In an anonymous April 1995 letter to *The New York Times*, this elusive terrorist demanded that the *Times*, or another major newspaper, publish a lengthy manifesto he had written, an article explaining his terrorist cause. Speaking as if he were the leader of a terrorist group, he wrote, "If you can get it published according to our requirements, we will permanently desist from [stop] terrorist activities."

And what would happen if no one would publish the Unabomber's manifesto? Then, the letter warned, "We expect we will be able to pack deadly bombs into ever smaller, lighter and more harmless looking packages. On the other hand, we believe we will be able to make bombs much [more powerful] than any we've made before."[11]

The Unabomber's demands left newspaper editors with a difficult choice. Should they give the Unabomber the publicity he called for? If they did not, they might find themselves responsible for more victims later on. But publishing the manifesto did not guarantee anything. This terrorist could simply break his promise and resume his campaign of terror.

In September 1995, *The New York Times* and the

Washington Post printed the entire text of the Unabomber's 35,000-word manifesto. In his original letter to the *Times*, the Unabomber had summed up his terrorist cause: "Our more immediate goal, which we think may be attainable at some time during the next several decades, is the destruction of the world-wide industrial system."[12] The manifesto kept to the same theme. "The Industrial Revolution and its consequences have been a disaster for the human race," it began.[13]

David Kaczynski had not seen his brother Ted in many years, but when he read the manifesto in *The New York Times*, he remembered things his brother had written years ago. David dug up some old journals his brother had kept and letters he had written to newspapers. When David read them alongside the published manifesto, disturbing similarities immediately jumped out at him. Like the Unabomber's manifesto, his brother's writings used some of the same language and focused on what he called the evils of modern industrial society.

Reluctantly, David Kaczynski contacted the FBI, and the FBI arrested Ted Kaczynski in his Montana cabin. All the evidence they would need to eventually convict him was right there on the scene. Kaczynski's cabin was crammed with bomb-making materials, records of experiments he had performed over the years to perfect his letter and package bombs, and copies of his manifesto. Ted Kaczynski was tried and convicted and sentenced in 1998 to life in prison without possibility of parole.

The debate over how the news media in an open

WARNING!

Letter and Package Bomb Indicators

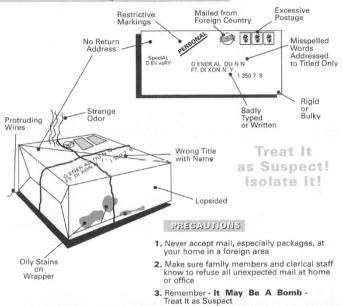

Restrictive Markings
Mailed from Foreign Country
Excessive Postage
No Return Address
PERSONAL
SpeclAL D Éli veRY
G ENER AL DU N N FT. DI XON N. Y.
1 350 7 8
Misspelled Words Addressed to Titled Only
Rigid or Bulky
Strange Odor
Protruding Wires
Badly Typed or Written
Wrong Title with Name
Lopsided
Oily Stains on Wrapper

Treat It as Suspect! Isolate It!

PRECAUTIONS

1. Never accept mail, especially packages, at your home in a foreign area

2. Make sure family members and clerical staff know to refuse all unexpected mail at home or office

3. Remember - **It May Be A Bomb** - Treat It as Suspect

LETTER AND PARCEL BOMB RECOGNITION POINTS

- Excessive Postage
- Incorrect Titles
- Titles but No Names
- Misspellings of Common Words
- Oily Stains or Discolorations
- No Return Address
- Excessive Weight
- Rigid Envelope

- Lopsided or Uneven Envelope
- Protruding Wires or Tinfoil
- Visual Distractions
- Foreign Mail, Air Mail and Special Delivery
- Restrictive Markings such as Confidential, Personal, etc.
- Hand Written or Poorly Typed Addresses
- Excessive Securing Material such as Masking Tape, String, etc.

FBI BOMB DATA CENTER (202) 324-2696

This FBI warning poster is meant to alert the American public to the threat of letter and package bombs.

society should handle the reporting of terrorist acts will continue. Each side will have arguments to back its beliefs. Both sides agree on one thing, though: All terrorists, no matter what cause they say they believe in, are destroyers. They destroy property and they injure and kill men, women, and children.

5

Victims of Terrorist Attacks

- Lord Mountbatten, a former British army officer fishing in Donegal Bay, off the coast of County Sligo, Ireland

- Seventeen kindergartners and their teacher trapped in an elevator between the thirty-sixth and thirty-fifth floors in New York's World Trade Center

- A student working in the engineering lab at the University of California, Berkeley, who is about to open a box

- A businessman in Nairobi, Kenya, getting up from his desk to see what caused a loud noise from the direction of the American Embassy

57

- Two American tourists hiking through a lush jungle in Uganda, East Africa, looking for rare gorillas

- Two brothers, ages two and three, who have just entered an Oklahoma City day-care center after kissing their mother goodbye

These people all had one thing in common. They were all victims of terrorist attacks while engaged in the activities listed above. Lord Mountbatten was killed by an IRA bomb. The schoolchildren and their teacher were saved by firefighters who cut a hole in the elevator. The University of Berkeley student's right arm and hand were permanently injured by a Unabomber package bomb. The Nairobi businessman was blown out onto the street but survived. The tourists were hacked to death by Rwandan rebels with knives, machetes, and hatchets. The two brothers were killed in the Oklahoma City bombing.

None of these people presented a direct threat of any kind to the terrorists who attacked them. They were all innocent victims.

Rescuing Victims

Rescue workers of all kinds rush in to help victims when a catastrophe such as the Oklahoma City bombing occurs. Everyone from architectural engineers to Boy Scouts may get involved.

Some rescue workers who helped in the aftermath of the Oklahoma City bombing were members of special organizations set up specially to deal with emergencies, such as the Federal Emergency

Rescue workers dig down into the wreckage of the Alfred P. Murrah Federal Building in search of survivors.

Management Agency (FEMA), the National Guard, the Red Cross, and local police, firefighters, and hospitals. Other rescuers were volunteers who swarmed into the city from all over the state and, eventually, surrounding states as well. Hundreds of doctors and nurses volunteered their services. A Boy Scout troop came to help with blood collection. Some people stood in line for up to six hours to donate blood. A sporting goods store shipped its entire supply of kneepads for the rescue workers who were crawling through the rubble.

Locating the Living

One of the most urgent tasks in a rescue effort is to locate victims trapped in the wreckage. The Oklahoma City bombing wreckage presented rescue workers with a particularly tricky and dangerous problem. The front of the Murrah Building had been blown away, and all nine floors had collapsed in on one another. The sagging remains of the building still standing were a potential death trap for anyone attempting to probe the wreckage for trapped survivors.

Architects and engineers came to help rescue workers figure out the safest way to proceed. Rescue equipment was rushed to the scene. Hydraulic lifts, cranes, and bulldozers were used to push, pull, and lift wreckage away from trapped victims. Search cameras with bright lights on long poles were maneuvered deep inside the wreckage to locate trapped victims. Thermal sensors were used to detect body

Police and firefighters rushed to the scene of the terrorist bombing in Oklahoma City, Oklahoma.

heat. Specially trained dogs sniffed the wreckage for signs of human life.

Sounds play a vital part in rescue operations. Rescuers could sometimes hear victims sobbing and calling out from deep inside the rubble. Rescue teams were equipped with listening devices sensitive enough to detect human heartbeats. Now and then a rescue team would call for silence. Helicopters were sent away, heavy equipment shut down, and radios switched off as rescuers held their breath and listened. "The idea is to get very quiet, don't even breathe, just drop the devices in and listen," a firefighter at the Oklahoma City site said.[1]

Identifying the Dead

The power of the explosion made identifying the dead a difficult task. Some bodies had been so violently torn apart that they had to be painstakingly pieced together and examined by medical experts before they could be identified. Forensic anthropologists looked for clues in the pieced-together skeletons. Forensic dentists looked for clues in dental work. Fingerprints, footprints, and X-rays were taken.

Meanwhile, family members spent anxious hours wondering whether loved ones were dead or alive. Twenty-four children, all between four months and five years of age, were in the day-care center on the ground floor of the Murrah Building when the bomb went off. Their parents waited for news at Children's Hospital. They wore strips of masking tape on which they had written the names of their children. They were hoping that someone would come and tell them that their children were there, among the ones being treated for injuries, and not among the dead.

Effects on Children

In Oklahoma City, ten children lost both parents in the blast. More than 150 people lost one parent, and nearly 40 percent of all the city's residents knew someone who was killed or injured.[2] A young man ready to start college had to drop his plans, get a job, and stay at home to take care of his younger brothers and sister when the blast left them orphans. "I didn't know it took all this responsibility. Paying bills, food, clothes," he said. "I put all my goals on hold."[3]

Witnesses at the scene recall seeing small children wandering around the parking lot outside the bombed building calling for their parents, and parents searching frantically for their children. One mother whose children survived the blast said, "When we got home, I turned on the television to watch, and it hit me that I had gone through this. We are lucky to have ended up a full family. I really feel for the parents of those lost children."[4]

Fear spread out from the bomb site all across the nation. A thousand miles away from Oklahoma City, in Chicago, Illinois, an eight-year-old girl heard the news of the blast on the radio. She turned to her mother and said, "I wonder what kind of a world I was born into."[5]

President Bill Clinton expressed his concern about how children of America might react to the bombing. He said he wanted them to know that "almost all the adults in this country are good people who love their children and love other children. And we're going to get through this."[6]

Effects on Adults

If you are a surviving victim, a terrorist attack is hard to put out of your mind. In New York, a man trapped in the World Trade Center after the bomb blew still recalls hearing voices all around him screaming, "God help us!"[7] A lawyer eating lunch in his World Trade Center office vividly remembers looking up to see his entire office shaking so hard that he thought he must be in the midst of an earthquake. Years later a man who witnessed the explosion said, "Not a day goes by when I don't think about it."[8]

Some survivors cannot help feeling guilty for still being alive when so many of their friends have died alongside them. A man in Nairobi lost forty coworkers in the embassy blast. Along with the other survivors in his company, he received psychological counseling to help him cope with the loss. "The ones who died were my friends," he said. "I had known them all for years."[9]

Some of the Unabomber's letter-bomb victims suffered permanent physical injury. One was John Hauser. In 1985 he opened what turned out to be a package bomb, using his right hand. "My Air Force Academy ring, which had been on my right ring finger, shot six feet through the air and bounced off a wall. The impact was so strong, you could read the word ACADEMY in the plaster."[10]

Hauser was a college student who dreamed of becoming an Air Force pilot. His flying career ended that day. "I actually feel fortunate to be here, to be alive," he said. Hauser learned to write left-handed and went on to become a college professor. He remembers his old dream, though, whenever he hears planes flying overhead. It sounds like the planes are calling to him, and he thinks, "I'd give my right arm to get my right arm back."[11]

Victims of a terrorist's random violence cannot help wondering why this happened. "Why would somebody do this without considering the human consequences of his actions?" John Hauser wonders. "That's unimaginable to me. That's going to take quite a while to understand."[12]

Monuments to Victims of Terrorism

The World Trade Center and the U.S. Embassy at Dar es Salaam were eventually rebuilt. When the new American Embassy in Dar es Salaam opened in March of 1999, a Tanzanian official said, "To some, the blast still shakes their eardrums, to some the horrors and pains of the wounded or losing loved ones haunts their thoughts and grief."[13]

In Nairobi, the United States donated $300 million to the owners of the sixty buildings damaged by the embassy bombing to help them rebuild. The Nairobi embassy itself, damaged beyond repair, was torn down.

But it would not be forgotten. On February 3, 2000, the United States and Kenya announced that they would work together to raise $3.5 million to turn the site of the former embassy into a memorial park dedicated to the 213 people killed in the blast. The two nations issued a joint statement that read:

"This park is a monument to the human spirit,

Flowers and children's toys are attached to a fence outside the bombed Murrah Building, in honor of the victims.

which will not accept evil. On the very spot where so many Kenyans and Americans died, we consecrate this land as a living monument testifying against terrorism, and for civilization."[14]

On April 19, 2000, five years to the day after the Oklahoma City bombing, a memorial was dedicated on the site where the Alfred P. Murrah Federal Building once stood. On the site is a grassy hill where 168 empty chairs now stand. Each empty chair represents one of the bombing victims. The chairs are made of stone and bronze. The nineteen small ones represent the children killed in the blast.

6

Tracking Down Terrorists

When it comes to law enforcement authorities tracking down terrorists, the hunted have certain advantages over the hunters. The authorities are predictable; they must operate within the law. Terrorists are unpredictable. They are not bound by any laws, legal or moral. Terrorists strike when and where and whom they please, and they operate in secrecy. Unless the authorities have been tipped off in advance about their plans of attack, terrorists have a running head start in the hunt.

68

The Hunted

Terrorists have hideouts waiting for them after they have staged an attack. Sometimes they run to safe houses (houses or apartments that are secure to hide in). While headquartered in these safe houses, terrorists lead a quiet life, keeping to themselves so they will not arouse suspicion as they plan their next attack.

Sometimes terrorists hide out in areas where the authorities cannot get to them even if they know where the terrorists have gone. The South Armagh borderlands, where Northern Ireland and the Republic of Ireland meet, is a notorious hideout for IRA terrorists. Most of the local inhabitants are IRA sympathizers. Snipers and land mines along the local roads keep British police and soldiers from daring to enter the area.

Some terrorists enjoy the luxury of entire nations in which to hide out. Also known as safe havens, these nations have helped finance the terrorists' operations. Nations known to provide havens for terrorists include Iran, Libya, the Sudan, and Afghanistan.

The Hunters

The FBI is responsible for tracking down terrorists who victimize American citizens within the United States and anywhere else around the world. Recently retired FBI director Louis Freeh stated that the bureau "has no higher priority than to combat terrorism; to prevent it where possible; and where prevention fails, to apprehend the terrorists and to do everything within the law to work for conviction and the most severe sentences."[1]

The FBI uses a variety of methods to help track down terrorists, from using sophisticated computer technology to questioning potential witnesses by going door-to-door. Computer databases and telecommunications networks give agents quick access to nationwide records of fingerprints, driver's licenses, passports, visas, hotel and motel reservations, airline passenger lists, and a wealth of other information. The bureau looks for help from the public by publishing names, descriptions, and photographs of suspects wanted for terrorist crimes on its Web site. The bureau also offers rewards for tips leading to the capture of suspected terrorists. Sometimes these tips lead to an actual capture.

Case Study: Kathleen Soliah, a.k.a. Sara Jane Olson

In one memorable case, the FBI tracked down a suspected terrorist through a network television program. The suspect, Kathleen Soliah, joined a counterculture terrorist group known as the Symbionese Liberation Army (SLA) in 1974. This group never had many members but became instantly famous when SLA members kidnapped Patricia Hearst in February 1974. Hearst's father was the president and editor of the *San Francisco Examiner* newspaper, and a prominent member of one of America's most influential media families.

Soliah joined the gang shortly after the Hearst kidnapping. During the next three years she allegedly took part in armed robberies and bombings. Most of the SLA members were caught in 1975. But Soliah eluded capture and went into hiding. Soliah was wanted for allegedly planting pipe bombs, which never exploded, under police squad cars.

Kathleen Soliah remained on the FBI's list of terrorist suspects for the next twenty-four years. A reward of $20,000 was offered for information leading to her capture. She managed to elude authorities until May of 1999, the twenty-fifth anniversary of the Hearst kidnapping, when pictures of Soliah were shown on *America's Most Wanted*, a Fox Network television show. Viewers with information on Soliah's whereabouts were told to phone the FBI. Tips came in that led agents to a suburb of St. Paul, Minnesota.

There they found a woman who called herself Sara Jane Olson. Olson, fifty-three, was a well-respected St. Paul resident, wife of a prominent doctor and mother of three daughters, active in local politics and charity work. Investigations by local police officers and FBI agents showed that viewers who had phoned in tips were right: Sara Jane Olson was actually Kathleen Soliah. The former SLA member's twenty-five years of hiding came to an end on June 16, 1999, when an FBI agent took her into custody near her home. "FBI, Kathleen," he said. "It's over."[2] Soliah was due to stand trial sometime in 2000.

Case Study: The World Trade Center Bombers

In the case of the World Trade Center bombers, FBI agents used computer databases and thorough detective work to bring four terrorists to justice. They also had some help from the terrorists themselves.

A painstaking search of the World Trade Center wreckage led to the discovery of a three-foot piece of metal from the body of a van. It was one of the axles, charred and twisted from the blast. A series of numbers were stamped on the axle. This was the van's vehicle identification number (VIN), a code to help police trace stolen or wrecked vehicles. Each car, van, and truck has its own VIN number stamped on different parts of the body, giving the vehicle's make, model, and year. The National Insurance Crime Bureau (NICB) in Dallas, Texas, keeps a nationwide registry of VIN numbers and their owners. A quick check of the VIN computer database matched the number on the twisted axle to a Ford Econoline E–350 van that had been sold to Ryder Truck Rental Company in Alabama.

A Ryder representative told the FBI that the van had been rented from the Jersey City, New Jersey, office. When the FBI contacted that office, they learned that the man who had rented the van three days before had just stopped in to collect his deposit. He was Mohammed Salameh, twenty-five, an illegal immigrant from Jordan. Salameh would have been wise to forget about collecting the deposit and to flee immediately after the bombing. Instead, he returned to the Ryder office, claiming that the van had been stolen and demanding his $400 deposit back. The Ryder people told Salameh that they would have to see a police report on the theft first, and he had left in anger just a few hours before the FBI call.

Incredibly, Salameh returned to the Ryder office on Monday, March 4, again demanding his $400 back. This time, the FBI was waiting for him. Salameh left the Ryder office in handcuffs.

Mohammed Salameh was one of four men caught and convicted of the World Trade Center bombing following a four-year worldwide manhunt. The man convicted of planning the attack, Ramzi Ahmed Yousef, was eventually tracked down and captured by FBI agents in Islamabad, Pakistan. He was living in a guesthouse called *Su Casa*, which Osama bin Laden kept as a safe house for terrorists to use. Yousef's fingerprints were found on a bomb manual

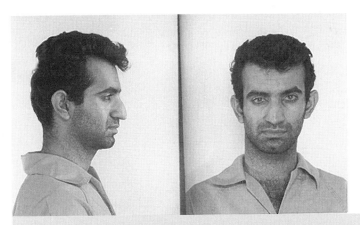

Ramzi Ahmed Yousef was convicted of masterminding the 1993 bombing of the New York World Trade Center.

in the Jersey City apartment where the conspiracy was planned. The driver of the van, Eyad Ismoil, was captured in Jordan. He also had left behind an incriminating fingerprint. It was found on a page of a phone book where he had torn out a coupon for a Ryder rental discount.

The FBI's early suspicions that the bombing had been carried out by a gang of extremist Muslim terrorists angry at the United States for its support of Israel had proved correct. Through a combination of sophisticated technology, determined detective work, and terrorist mistakes, agents tracked the bombers down.

Case Study: The Oklahoma City Bombing

A similar combination of hard work and luck figured into the capture and conviction of Timothy McVeigh. Like Salameh, McVeigh made fatal mistakes. He was already on the road when the bomb went off, headed north. But his getaway car, a Mercury Marquis, had no rear license plate. McVeigh never said whether this was a fatal blunder on his part or deliberate. Members of militias and hate groups are known to drive without license plates deliberately, as a form of protest against paying taxes to the government.

Deliberate or not, the lack of plates caught the attention of an Oklahoma state trooper, who pulled McVeigh over near the town of Billings. It was a routine traffic stop until the trooper noticed the shoulder harness that McVeigh wore underneath his left arm. Tucked into it was a semiautomatic pistol loaded with hollow-point "cop killer" bullets, specially made to mushroom inside a person's body on contact. This was no longer a routine traffic stop. The trooper put McVeigh under arrest for carrying a concealed weapon.

The jail was in the town of Perry, Oklahoma. While the nationwide manhunt went on for the Oklahoma City bomber, McVeigh sat quietly in his cell, waiting to be brought before a judge. Two days later he was about to get his wish. McVeigh was only minutes short of being set free on bail that Friday morning when the district attorney received a phone call from the FBI telling him to hold on to his prisoner.

McVeigh might have gotten away that morning if not for something that had fallen from the sky. Just before the bomb went off Wednesday morning, Richard Nichols was walking to his car with his wife. The Nichols's Ford Festiva was parked kitty-corner from the Murrah Building. Then, Nichols says, "there was a horrific explosion" as McVeigh's bomb blew. "All this stuff was coming down," Nichols said. And he saw "this humongous object" coming at him from the direction of the Murrah Building, spinning in space like a boomerang and giving off a whirring noise.[3] Nichols pushed his wife aside just as the object hit their car, smashing the windshield and lifting the vehicle into the air.

The humongous spinning object was the rear axle from the Ryder truck that had housed McVeigh's bomb. It weighed 250 pounds, and it had been hurled 575 feet through the air before crashing into the Nichols's Festiva.[4]

FBI agents found the VIN number on the axle and traced it to Elliott's Body Shop in Junction City, Kansas. The truck had been rented by a man calling himself Robert Kling. The rental agent gave the FBI a description of Kling, which an FBI artist turned into a composite sketch. The FBI distributed copies of the sketch, along with a description of the truck, to people in the area and to newspapers and television stations nationwide. When the owner of the Dreamland Motel in Junction City saw the sketch the night after the bombing, he told the FBI that a man who matched it had recently registered there under the name Timothy McVeigh. That same night an old friend of McVeigh's from Buffalo, New York, saw the sketch on television and immediately phoned the FBI, confirming McVeigh's identity.

A national crime computer check turned up McVeigh's name and where he was: in the Perry, Oklahoma, jail on gun and traffic charges. Instead of leaving on bail that morning, McVeigh was taken into custody by the FBI.

Case Study: The 1998 Embassy Bombings

The U.S. embassy bombings in Africa in 1998 presented the FBI with a different set of problems. When the FBI is going after terrorists who have struck on United States soil, agents operate on familiar ground. They know they can rely on nationwide computer databases, the local police, the media, and the public to help them track down terrorists.

Things are different outside of the United States.

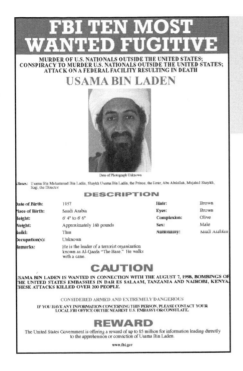

This wanted poster for Osama bin Laden can be found on the FBI's Internet site. Note that the FBI spells his name "Usama," as it is sometimes written.

Immediately after the blasts, 251 FBI agents, along with explosives experts from the ATF, were sent to east Africa. Their first job was to sift through the rubble for clues. The FBI agents assigned to Kenya were greeted with a disheartening sight. The rear parking lot, where the bomb had gone off, had already been bulldozed and much of the debris hauled away.

Agents still managed to locate pieces of the exploded truck in the planeloads of debris hauled back to Washington for examination. Meanwhile, agents interviewed over seven hundred Kenyans in the first few days alone. Agents did the same in Tanzania.

By January 2000, seventeen people had been charged with conspiracy in the bombings. All were extremist Muslims, and five were charged with having worked directly with Osama bin Laden at one time or another. One had served as bin Laden's manager of finances. Another had been his personal secretary, and another was leader of the Kenyan branch of bin Laden's al Qaeda terrorist organization. Suspect Mohammed Saddiq Odeh called bin Laden his spiritual guide and supreme commander in the Islamic holy war against the United States.

None of these men would confirm that bin Laden worked with him, but American officials offered a $5 million reward for information leading to bin Laden's capture. They want to bring him to the United States to stand trial. He has been charged with having masterminded the World Trade Center bombing as well as with the bombings in Africa. Bin Laden also has been charged with planning a series of attacks on Americans both within the United States and in the Middle East during the year 2000 millennium celebrations.

Federal law permits the United States to bring charges against anyone who attempts or conspires to murder Americans anywhere in world, but American authorities do not always have the right to pursue a suspect outside of United States borders. FBI agents believe that bin Laden is headquartered in a town in Afghanistan near the Pakistan border, but they are not allowed to cross the border to hunt for him. Most of Afghanistan is ruled by a Muslim militia known as the Taliban, and the Taliban have given bin Laden the use of their nation as a safe haven.

In the meantime, bin Laden and other terrorist leaders are believed to be planning new attacks on Americans at home and abroad.

7

Counterterrorism

According to recently retired FBI director Louis Freeh, counterterrorism means "we get there before the bomb goes off, before the plane is hijacked, before innocent Americans lose their lives."[1] Freeh said that stopping terrorism on American soil is the FBI's number one goal, and steady increases in government funding for counterterrorism prove him right. In 1997 the federal government spent $6.7 billion on counter- terrorism activities. By the year 2000 that figure had jumped to $10 billion.[2] In 1993 there were 550 FBI agents devoted to counterterrorism. By 2000 there were more than 1,300.[3] According to a U.S.

State Department report, the number of international terrorist attacks rose from 274 in 1998 to 392 in 1999. But the number of people killed or wounded in these attacks actually fell sharply, from 6,693 to 939.[4]

Even with dedication, determination, and plenty of dollars, stopping terrorism is a difficult matter. Terrorists are unpredictable. One of their chief strategies is surprise. How can the authorities possibly be on the spot to prevent the next attack if they do not know where, when, or how the attack is coming?

When he was director of the FBI, Louis Freeh led the United States's counterterrorism activities during a time of increased international terrorism.

Gathering Intelligence

First, authorities must be able to predict terrorist plans. To do this, they must find ways to listen in on secret terrorist communications. Intercepting secret information is known as gathering intelligence.

Some of this intelligence comes from orbiting space satellites that monitor electronic signals and take pictures from high above Earth. A secret intelligence operation known by the code name ECHELON uses these satellites along with a series of intercepting stations positioned all around the world. These stations collect radio, telephone, satellite, and computer communications worldwide. This secret intelligence operation is capable of capturing virtually every telephone call and e-mail message sent anywhere in the world.

This collected information is then fed into ultrapowerful computers at National Security Agency (NSA) headquarters in Fort Meade, Maryland. Like Internet search engines, these computers are programmed to search for certain key words and phrases that might signal terrorist activity. The computers separate out communications containing these key words and phrases and send them on to the Central Intelligence Agency (CIA), the FBI, and other government agencies for analysis.

Intelligence agencies in other countries routinely share their information with the United States. Washington claims that between 1998 and 2000, the information collected by intelligence agencies in the United States and around the world led to the breaking up of more than two dozen of Osama bin Laden's al Qaeda terrorist cells.[5]

Monitoring Entry Points

Knowing that terrorists are likely to strike in advance is one thing; actually stopping them is another. Often authorities have only a general idea of when and where trouble is brewing. Then they must put special counterterrorism strategies into action.

One of these strategies focuses on points of entry. The United States has always been a nation that welcomes immigrants and visitors. Closed societies, such as Cuba and Afghanistan, put more restrictions on who is allowed to visit their nation. Compared with these closed societies, gaining legal entry to the United States is relatively easy. The thousands of miles of borderland with Canada and Mexico also make it difficult for authorities to monitor who comes into and leaves the country.

The United States has 301 ports of entry, places where people may legally enter and leave the country. These ports and borders are watched over by agents from the ATF, U.S. Customs, and the U.S. Border Patrol. Their job is to check anyone or anything that appears suspicious. When authorities have reason to believe that a terrorist attack is about to take place, these agents are put on high alert. This high-alert plan went into effect during the last month of 1999, and the strategy worked.

Case Study: The Millennium Terror

NSSE stands for National Security Special Event, an event that calls for extraordinary precautions. Authorities in the United States and the Middle East decided that the coming of the year 2000 was one of these special events. Not only did it mark the new millennium, this was also the time of Ramadan, the most important Muslim religious holiday. U.S. government officials predicted that terrorist groups linked to Osama bin Laden could be planning as many as fifteen separate violent attacks against American and Israeli citizens around the world. So government officials drew up a blueprint for action, the "Millennium Threats Plan," and security forces were put on special alert.

In the Middle East, these special precautions paid off on December 1, when authorities in Amman, Jordan, arrested thirteen men. Files from the suspects' computers contained instructions on how to build bombs and information about terrorist training camps in Afghanistan. The thirteen were charged with planning to use AK–47 rifles to gun down tourists at an American hotel, the American Embassy, and three different tourist sites in Jordan on the eve of the millennium. Later, two more suspects were arrested. All fifteen suspects have been linked to Osama bin Laden. Their trial began in April 2000. If convicted, they face the death penalty.

Thirteen other suspects eluded capture. One of them was Abu Zubayduh, a key lieutenant of Osama bin Laden. Zubayduh was in charge of communications between al Qaeda and other terrorist groups around the world.

One of these groups consisted of four Algerians living in Canada. They too had terrorist plans for the millennium. Their target was the United States. The head of the Algerian group was Ahmed Ressam. Authorities believe Ressam spent time in a bin Laden terrorist camp known for training Algerians. On December 14, Ressam loaded bomb-making materials into the trunk of his rented Chrysler. He carried military explosives and homemade detonators made of circuit boards connecting wristwatches to 9–volt detonating devices. Ressam drove the car onto a ferry that took him from Victoria, British Columbia, to Port Angeles, Washington, northwest of Seattle.

Under normal circumstances Ressam might have made it across the Canadian border into the United States. But a customs agent, on high alert, spotted Ressam's hands shaking on the steering wheel. She told him to pull over and open the trunk.

Ressam fled on foot. He was captured a few blocks away and arrested. After the arrest, FBI and CIA agents using ECHELON data discovered links between the millennium bomb plots in the United States and Jordan and links between those plots and Osama bin Laden.

Special millennium precautions were taken all across the United States and around the world. On December 11, the State Department issued a Worldwide Travel Caution for U.S. citizens traveling abroad, since they were likely targets of terrorism. Travelers were advised to "avoid large crowds and gatherings, keep a low profile, and vary routes and times of all required travel."[6] The government conducted special emergency drills in twenty-seven cities. After Ressam's arrest, the mayor of Seattle, Washington, canceled that city's millennium celebration. On New Year's Eve in New York City's Times Square, some ten thousand policemen mingled with the crowds while bomb-sniffing dogs patrolled the city's underground tunnels.

There were no terrorist attacks involving Americans during the millennium. But what happens when authorities fail to heed warnings of imminent terrorist attacks?

Case Study: The Nairobi Embassy Bombing

In November of 1997, nine months before the 1998 embassy bombings in Africa, an Egyptian named Mustafa Mamoud Ahmed walked into the American Embassy in Nairobi, Kenya, and asked to see American officials. He had come to deliver an ominous warning. Muslim extremists were planning to load a truck with bombs and detonate them inside the embassy's underground parking garage, he warned. Ahmed said that he knew these terrorists personally. He had even taken surveillance photos of the embassy for them. But now he had second thoughts. He wanted to stop these men from committing this terrible crime.

Officials in Nairobi put the embassy on a high-alert status for several weeks after Ahmed's visit. Meanwhile, a report was sent to Washington, D.C. After reviewing the report, CIA officials decided that

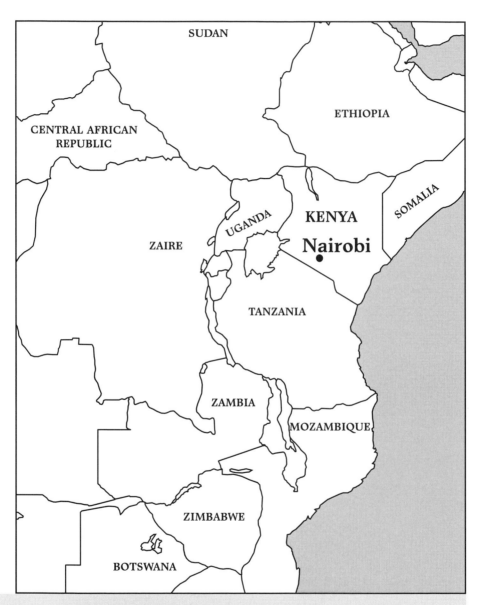

Better preparation for a terrorist attack might have prevented the loss of life and damage to property from the 1998 embassy bombing in Nairobi.

Ahmed was unreliable. They discounted his warning, and security at the Nairobi embassy was returned to normal.

After American officials alerted Kenyan authorities to Ahmed, he was deported, but security at the embassy was kept at a normal level. In August of 1998 the embassy was bombed in exactly the way that Ahmed had warned American officials it would be bombed nine months earlier. Ahmed was later arrested and charged with conspiracy in the embassy bombings. He was also linked with Osama bin Laden.

Ignoring Ahmed's warning was not the only mistake that U.S. officials made in the Nairobi bombing. A U.S. State Department investigation concluded that embassy personnel in both Nairobi and Dar es Salaam should have been prepared to deal with a terrorist attack, but they had not been properly trained.[7] In Nairobi, when the terrorist's grenade exploded, all embassy employees should have known to immediately drop to the floor. That way they would have been out of the way of flying glass when the bomb exploded moments later. Instead, they rushed to the windows. Some people were decapitated, while others were seriously injured by flying glass hitting them in the chest and face.

The investigation noted other mistakes. Embassy guards had never been trained in detecting car bombs. The embassy had no special radio frequency dedicated to security. The embassy building should have been set back away from the road and away from other buildings at least one hundred feet, but it was not. The panel concluded that this was "an institutional failure of the Department of State and embassies under its direction to recognize threats posed by transnational terrorism and vehicle bombs."[8]

In February 2000, President Bill Clinton asked Congress for a billion dollars to improve U.S. embassy security around the world and a billion more over each of the next three years. Besides improving security, President Clinton also decided to retaliate.

Striking Back

Retaliation is another strategy for preventing terrorism. By punishing the terrorists, you discourage them from striking again. The strategy sounds simple, but the execution can be complex and the results can be unexpected.

Terrorists are by nature secretive and elusive. Their bases of operation are hard to pinpoint. You cannot strike back if you cannot find the target, and Osama bin Laden's bases of operation have always been hard to find. But Clinton was determined to send a message to bin Laden in particular and terrorists in general. He decided to launch missile attacks, so he had his advisors draw up a list of twenty possible targets in three different countries.

Several of bin Laden's terrorist camps in Afghanistan were chosen. The other target was a chemical plant in Al Shifa in the East African nation of Sudan. This last target was a controversial one. In December 1997 a CIA agent had collected a soil sample a short distance from the plant. An analysis suggested that the soil contained traces of a chemical sometimes used to produce a deadly nerve gas. The Al Shifa plant was supposed to be manufacturing medicines, but American authorities suspected that it was being used by bin Laden to prepare for terrorist attacks.

But results of the soil analysis were not conclusive, and there was no hard evidence showing that the plant posed a direct threat to the United States. Some U.S. officials favored the Al Shifa strike, anyway. They strongly suspected that bin Laden was organizing a deadly chemical weapons attack against the United States, and that this plant was being used to manufacture those weapons.

But other officials were skeptical. CIA director George Tenet warned that no one had come up with any hard evidence linking the Al Shifa plant to bin Laden. A report issued by the State Department Bureau of Intelligence and Research raised the same doubts.

Still, the majority of Clinton's advisors believed they had enough evidence to proceed with the strike. On August 20, 1998, thirteen days after the embassy bombings, the United States launched cruise missile attacks against several of bin Laden's terrorist camps in Afghanistan and against the Al Shifa plant.

The plant was destroyed. Reporters visiting the ruined building saw no signs to indicate that chemical weapons had ever been produced at the plant. And Western engineers who had worked at the plant told reporters that medicines had been manufactured there, not weapons. But U.S. officials insisted that the plant was a legitimate target of retaliation because it had been manufacturing chemical weapons for bin Laden.

Draining the Swamp

U.S. officials had hoped that the cruise missile attacks on bin Laden's Afghanistan camps would kill bin Laden himself, but al Qaeda's leader survived. Hitting these terrorist camps was part of a larger strategy for dealing with terrorists known as draining the swamp—leaving terrorists no place to hide. U.S. Secretary of State Madeleine Albright has called for "international agreements and cooperation that will leave terrorists with no place to run, hide, do their dirty work, or stash their assets."[9]

The United Nations (UN) is dedicated to international peace and security. The 185 member nations have agreed to cooperate in preventing terrorist acts and keeping terrorists out of their territories. On October 15, 1999, the UN passed Resolution 1267, imposing strict economic sanctions against Afghanistan.[10] Among these sanctions is a ban on flights into and out of that nation. The ruling Taliban militia was told that before the sanctions could be lifted, it must turn bin Laden over to the United States for trial. By passing Resolution 1267, the UN succeeded in isolating Afghanistan from most of the rest of the world, in the hope that its leaders would be persuaded to join the worldwide war against terrorism.

This war against terrorism has always been serious. But with recent changes in weapons and communications technologies, terrorism poses new kinds of threats.

8

The Future of Terrorism

On the morning of March 19, 1995, a man boarded a Tokyo, Japan, subway car. The man wore a surgical mask, but the other riders barely noticed. It was hay fever season in Japan, and lots of hay fever sufferers wore masks just like his to filter irritating pollen from the air. But that was not why this man was wearing the mask.

The man in the mask sat down and put a package on the seat beside him. No one was alarmed when he picked up the package and set it down on the floor next to him, then poked it with his umbrella. And no one paid much attention when he exited the train at the next station, leaving the package behind.

As the train rolled on, a pool of oily liquid began forming around the punctured package, and riders in the car began feeling strange. Something was wrong with the air. Something was making it hard to breathe. Something was choking their lungs and stinging their eyes.

Then they started falling to the floor, and then they began to die. Three women fell in a heap clinging to one another. They made no sound. The deadly gas rising up out of the punctured package on the floor had taken their breath away before they could cry for help.

They had been killed by sarin, a gas that attacks the nervous system, skin, and blood. The terrorists had planted sarin gas bombs on four other trains that March morning. A total of twelve people died and thousands were injured.[1] Many more might have died. If the sarin gas had spread throughout the subway system, as the terrorists had planned, it would have killed thousands.

Superterrorists

The Tokyo subway gas attack was not carried out by traditional terrorists. Traditional terrorists seek revenge against the people and institutions that they believe have hurt them and their cause. They are hungry for power and change. Timothy McVeigh, the Oklahoma City bomber, hoped to inspire an entire nation to rise up against a government that he believed had betrayed the American people. Ted Kaczynski, the Unabomber, hoped to rid the world of modern technology, which he believed had ruined both the natural world and human society. The men who bombed the World Trade Center and the American embassies in Africa hoped to pressure the U.S. government into ending its support for Israel. Each of these traditional terrorists was out to change the world in his own way.

The ten terrorists who left the packages of nerve gas on the Tokyo subway that March morning were not traditional terrorists. For years the religious cult to which they belonged, Aum Shinrikyo, had been secretly stockpiling weapons of mass destruction. They were not trying to pressure the Japanese government into changing its policies. Their ultimate goal was not to change the world but to end it.

The Aum Shinrikyo subway gassing was the only attack carried out by a superterrorist group, a group using weapons of mass destruction, in the twentieth century. But some government officials believe there are more to come. Then Secretary of Defense William Cohen said that it was not a matter of whether large-scale superterrorist attacks would occur but when. President Bill Clinton warned that the use of biological and chemical weapons was highly likely in the twenty-first century. The threat of a superterrorist attack "keeps me awake at night," he said.[2]

Weapons of Mass Destruction

What keeps some government officials awake at night is the thought of weapons of mass destruction falling into the hands of people eager to use them. Conventional weapons, bullets or bombs, do most of their damage in a few seconds. Weapons of mass destruction (WMD) are different. These weapons have the power to keep on killing, spreading death in all directions and making entire regions of the world uninhabitable for days, weeks, even months on end.

Weapons of mass destruction fall into three classes: chemical, biological, and nuclear. Chemical weapons are manmade compounds that attack the nervous system, skin, and blood. The sarin gas used by the Aum Shinrikyo terrorists was a chemical weapon, and the cult had the capacity to manufacture a great deal more of it. When police raided the cult's headquarters following the attack, they uncovered tons of chemicals used in the manufacture of sarin gas.

While chemical weapons are made in laboratories, biological weapons are found in nature. One of these biological weapons is anthrax, an infectious bacterial disease that comes from infected animals such as cattle. Anthrax germs can be taken from nature and made to multiply in a laboratory, so that a few germs can be developed into a great many.

According to the U.S. Department of Defense, anthrax is the easiest biological weapon to get hold of and turn into a weapon. It can be spread by airborne spores, single cells that can grow into living organisms. These spores can easily be spread in the air over a large area. If breathed in and not treated immediately, anthrax spores nearly always cause death. In February 1999, an American microbiologist, Larry Wayne Harris, was arrested for conspiring to develop anthrax germs. Harris claimed that he had gathered anthrax spores from the graves of dead cows. Harris also claimed that he could get hold of germs that cause two other highly contagious deadly diseases, cholera and bubonic plague. "Sure," Harris told a television journalist, "it's very easy." Amy Smithson, an expert on terrorism and weapons of mass destruction, agreed. "If you have some technical skills," she said, "you can produce them cheaply."[3]

A U.S. Department of Defense document states: "Anthrax is a deadly biological warfare agent that at least ten nations, including North Korea and Iraq, are known to possess or have in development."[4] Since all members of the United States Armed Forces could be sent to those nations for active duty, they are being vaccinated to protect them against anthrax.

Nuclear weapons are the third and deadliest class of weapons of mass destruction. Could a terrorist group actually manufacture a homemade nuclear bomb? In the late 1970s, a Massachusetts Institute of Technology chemistry student set out to see if an amateur could design a nuclear bomb using only information available to the general public. After five weeks of work, he submitted his finished design to a nuclear weapons expert. If the bomb had actually been made, it would have been the size of a desk and it would have weighed between 550 and 1,000 pounds. The expert said that a bomb built from the student's design would work.

But were the materials for such a bomb available to the average person? In 1996, seventeen scientists at Los Alamos nuclear weapons laboratory in New

Mexico set out to answer this question. Using only materials that could be found at an electronics store and the kind of nuclear fuel that might be available illegally, on the black market, they managed to put together a dozen workable nuclear bombs.

Lessons Learned

The Aum Shinrikyo attack showed us that the face of international terrorism was changing. A new kind of terrorist was out there now with new kinds of weapons. The Report of the National Commission on Terrorism stated that the United States "must develop and continuously refine sound counterterrorism policies appropriate to the rapidly changing world around us."[5]

The 1998 embassy bombings reminded us that Americans were still prime targets in other parts of the world. The report also stated, "Terrorists attack American targets more often than those of any other country. America's pre-eminent [leading] role in the world guarantees that this will continue to be the case, and the threat of attacks creating massive casualties is growing."[6]

Before the World Trade Center bombing, in 1993, there had never been a major terrorist attack on U.S. soil. Before the Oklahoma City bombing, in 1995, there had never been a major terrorist attack by an American citizen against his own nation. These attacks, along with the Unabomber's long string of mail-bomb attacks, showed us that terrorism had become a part of life in America, a force that had to be dealt with. And worse was yet to come.

World Trade Center and Pentagon Attacked

At 8:46 A.M. on September 11, 2001, Americans were stunned to learn that a Boeing 767 airliner had crashed into the north tower of the 110-story World Trade Center in New York City. But that was only the beginning. Seventeen minutes later, another 767 hit the Trade Center's south tower. At 9:40 A.M., a third airliner hit the west side of the Pentagon, headquarters for the U.S. armed forces, in Washington, D.C. A fourth airliner crashed near an abandoned mineshaft in Shanksville, Pennsylvania, at 10:10 A.M. All four planes had been hijacked by terrorists, who took control from the pilots and turned the planes into deadly weapons. The first three planes had reached their targets. On the fourth, the passengers had apparently overcome the hijackers and caused the plane to crash in an uninhabited area.[7]

The World Trade Center was quickly aflame from the jet fuel that spilled out of the airliners. While many people below the points of impact on the upper floors were able to escape, most of those above were trapped.

About 130,000 people worked in or visited the World Trade Center each day. As survivors fled the site by the thousands, firefighters, police, and rescue workers rushed in to control the fire, help the injured, and search for survivors. Then, less than two hours after the first crash, both towers collapsed.

Several smaller buildings adjacent to the towers also collapsed. Dust and smoke filled the air for blocks. Thousands of people, including hundreds of rescue workers, became victims. Rescue and recovery efforts continued for weeks, with very few people recovered alive.

The attack on the World Trade Center killed about three thousand people. The attack on the Pentagon killed nearly two hundred people, including sixty-four passengers and crew on the plane. The plane crash in Pennsylvania killed all forty-five passengers and crew on board but no one on the ground.[8]

Response to the Attack

As the world watched, workers sifted through the rubble, and Americans lined up to give blood and

The west side of the Pentagon, the headquarters for the U.S. military, was hit by a Boeing 757 with sixty-four people aboard.

provide supplies to those devastated by the attacks. Meanwhile, U.S. leaders formulated a response. President George W. Bush declared, "The deliberate and deadly attacks that were carried out against our country were more than acts of terror. They were acts of war."[9] He vowed to oppose the terrorists by improving intelligence and security measures. With this in mind, Attorney General John Ashcroft proposed changes in laws concerning surveillance and immigration that would make it easier for authorities to find and hold suspected terrorists. Bush also said the United States would use military force in countries that housed terrorist networks, and other nations offered their support.

Authorities pieced together evidence and identified the suicide hijackers in the four airliners. The terrorists held passports from several different countries—Saudi Arabia, Lebanon, and the United Arab Emirates—and they had been living in the United States, where some had received pilot training.

Evidence pointed to Osama bin Laden and his al Qaeda organization as having funded and planned the attacks. But capturing or eliminating bin Laden and members of his network would not eliminate terrorism. Terrorism is a harsh reality that is not going away. Acts of terrorism, such as the September 11, 2001, attacks, are designed to make us feel confused, anxious, vulnerable, and outraged. Most of us would rather not think about it, but terrorism must be faced and dealt with. It is an ongoing threat to peace and security that cannot be ignored.

Chapter Notes

Chapter 1. What Is a Terrorist?

1. Bob Drogin, "Embassy Security Still Not Enough?" *Los Angeles Times*, April 26, 2000, <seattletimes. nwsource.com/news/nation-world/html98/ emba27_20000427.html> (August 28, 2000).

2. "Domestic Terrorism Program." U.S. Federal Bureau of Investigation, n.d., <www.fbi.gov/contact/fo/ norfolk/domterr.htm> (August 22, 2000)

3. Michael Sheehan, "Post-Millennium Terrorism Review," U.S. Department of State, February 10, 2000, <www.state.gov/www/policy_remarks/2000/000210_ sheehan_brookings.html> (July 2, 2000).

4. Transcript of "The Terrorist and the Superpower: Interview with Osama Bin Laden," *Frontline* (PBS television), May 1998, <www.pbs.org/wgbh/pages/ frontline/shows/binladen/who/interview.html> (August 12, 2000).

5. Ibid.

6. Sheehan.

Chapter 2. Terrorism Involving Americans

1. David Mark Chalmers, *Hooded Americanism: The History of the Ku Klux Klan* (Durham, North Carolina: Duke University Press, 1987), p. 9.

2. "Ku Klux Klan," Encyclopedia Britannica Online, n.d., <http://www.search.eb.com/bol/topic?eu=47396 &sctn=1&pm=1> (September 22, 1999).

3. Alexander Chancellor, "The Fun Resumes," *Slate Magazine*, February 24, 2000, <slate.msn.com/ InterNatPapers/00-02-24/InterNatPapers.asp> (August 2, 2000).

4. Todd Gitlin, *The Sixties: Years of Hope, Days of Rage* (New York: Bantam Books, 1987), p. 392.

5. Lester A. Sobel, ed., *Political Terrorism* (New York: Facts on File, 1975), p. 188.

6. Joseph P. Fried, "Inquiry Reopened on F.A.L.N. Actions," *The New York Times*, December 6, 1981, p. 49.

7. David A. Vise and Lorraine Adams, "FALN a Threat, Reno Says," *Washington Post*, October 21, 1999, <www.jonathanpollard.org/1999/102199c.htm> (August 22, 2000).

8. Michael Sheehan, "The Battle Against Terrorism: Report from the Administration," The Washington Institute for Near East Policy, n.d., <www.washingtoninstitute.org/media/sheehan.htm> (May 1, 2000).

9. Jay Robert Nash, *Terrorism in the 20th Century* (New York: M. Evans and Company, 1998), p. 247.

10. Ken Adelman, "When America Was Held Hostage," *Wall Street Journal*, November 4, 1999, p. A30.

11. Russell Watson, "The Hunt Begins," *Newsweek*, March 8, 1993, p. 23.

12. Ibid., p. 22.

13. Louis Freeh, "Ensuring Public Safety and National Security Under the Rule of Law: A Report to the American People on the Work of the FBI 1993–1998," Federal Bureau of Investigation, n.d., <www.fbi.gov/library/5-year/5YR_report_.PDF> (June 28, 2000).

14. Joe Klein, "The Nervous '90s," *Newsweek*, May 1, 1995, p. 58.

Chapter 3. How Terrorists See the World

1. John George and Laird M. Wilcox, *American Extremists: Militias, Supremacists, Klansmen, Communists and Others* (Amherst, New York: Prometheus Books, 1996), p. 56.

2. Richard Falk, *Revolutionaries and Functionaries* (New York: E.P. Dutton, 1988), p. 85.

3. Richard Lacayo, "How Safe Is Safe?" *Time*, May 1, 1995, p. 71.

4. Jim Yardley, "5 Years After Terrorist Act, a Memorial to the 168 Victims," *The New York Times*, April 20, 2000, <www.nytinmes.com/library/national/042000oklahoma-bomb.html>(June 4, 2000).

5. Brandon M. Stickney, *All-American Monster: The Unauthorized Biography of Timothy McVeigh* (Amherst, New York: Prometheus Books, 1996), p. 117.

6. Ibid., p. 137.

7. Richard A. Serrano, *One of Ours: Timothy McVeigh and the Oklahoma City Bombing* (New York: Norton, 1998), p. 97.

Chapter 4. How Terrorists Operate

1. Alexander Chancellor, "The Fun Resumes," *Slate Magazine*, February 24, 2000, <slate.msn.com/InterNatPapers/00-02-24/InterNatPapers.asp> (July 12, 2000).

2. Jay Robert Nash, *Terrorism in the 20th Century: A Narrative Encyclopedia from the Anarchists Through the Weathermen, to the Unabomber* (New York: M. Evans and Company, 1998), p. 405.

3. Russell Watson, "The Hunt Begins," *Newsweek*, March 8, 1993, p. 25.

4. Benjamin Weiser, "Two Convicted in 1993 Plot to Blow Up Trade Center," *The New York Times,* November 13, 1997, <search1.nytimes.com/search/daily/bin/fastweb?getdoc+site+site+141479+1+wAAA+world%7Etrade%7Ecenter%7Ebomb> (November 10, 2000).

5. Christopher John Farley, "America's Bomb Culture," *Time*, May 8, 1995, p. 56.

6. Margaret O. Hyde and Elizabeth H. Forsyth, *Terrorism: A Special Kind of Violence* (New York: G. P. Putnam's Sons, 1987), p. 52.

7. "Total International Terrorist Attacks, 1979–1998," U.S. Department of State, n.d., <www.state.gov/www/global/terrorism/1998Report/u.gif> (June 28, 2000).

8. "Attack on the USS Cole," "C–4 Explosive Used in USS Cole Attack," <www.cnn.com/2000/US/11/01/cole.investigation>, "Security Tightened as Investigators in Yemen Receive Bomb Threat," <www.nytimes.com/2000/10/26/word/26WIRE-YEMEN.html>, "Yemen Reports Arrests of Foreign-Born Arabs in Cole Attack," <www.nytimes.com/2000/10/26/world/26SHIP.html> (November 15, 2000).

9. John O'Sullivan, "Deny Them Publicity," reprinted in Benjamin Netanyahu, ed., *Terrorism: How the West Can Defeat Domestic & International Terrorists* (New York: Farrar, Straus, & Giroux, 1995), p. 120.

10. "Lost in the Terrorist Theater," *Harper's*, October 1984, p. 58.

11. "Bombing in Sacramento: The Letter," *The New York Times*, April 26, 1995, p. A16.

12. Ibid.

13. Alston Chase, "Harvard and the Making of the Unabomber," *The Atlantic Monthly*, June 2000, p. 43.

Chapter 5. Victims of Terrorist Attacks

1. Nancy Gibbs, "The Blood of Innocents," *Time*, May 1, 1995, p. 61.

2. John Leland and Peter Annin, "The Orphans of Oklahoma City," *Newsweek*, April 22, 1996, p. 41.

3. Ibid., p. 42.

4. John Leland, "Why the Children?" *Newsweek*, May 1, 1995, p. 51.

5. Russell Watson, "It's a Scary World," *Newsweek*, May 1, 1995, p. 53.

6. Ibid.

7. Tom Mathews, Karen Breslau, Patrick Rogers, and Marc Peyser, "A Shaken City's Towering Inferno," *Newsweek*, March 8, 1993, p. 26.

8. Somini Sengupta, "Is There Relief in This? Yes. Is It Closed? I Doubt It," *The New York Times*, November 13, 1997, p. B5.

9. Cathy Jenkins, "Africa Picking Up the Pieces," *BBC News*, August 6, 1999, <news.bbc.co.uk/hi/english/world/africa/newsid_413000/413015.stm> (June 22, 2000).

10. John Hauser, "What the Unabomber Did to Me," Newsweek, April 15, 1996, p. 40.

11. Ibid.

12. Ibid.

13. Charles W. Corey, "New Interim U.S. Embassy Opened in Tanzania," United States Information Agency, March 2, 1999, <usinfo.state.gov/topical/pol/terror/99030202.htm> (August 4, 2000).

14. "August 7th Memorial Park," U.S. Department of State, February 3, 2000, <www.usembassy.state.gov/posts/ke1/wwwh1116.html> (November 17, 2000).

Chapter 6. Tracking Down Terrorists

1. Louis Freeh, "Ensuring Public Safety and National Security Under the Rule of Law: A Report to the American People on the Work of the FBI 1993–1998," Federal

Bureau of Investigation, n.d., <www.fbi.gov/library/ 5-year/1993-98/report5.htm#anchor213286> (November 15, 2000).

2. Phil McCombs, "A Wanted Woman," *Washington Post*, July 1, 1999, p. C01.

3. Richard A. Serrano, *One of Ours: Timothy McVeigh and the Oklahoma City Bombing* (New York: Norton, 1998), p. 188.

4. Ibid, pp. 188–189.

Chapter 7. Counterterrorism

1. Louis J. Freeh, "What Can Be Done About Terrorism?" reprinted in Frank McGuckin, ed., *Terrorism in the United States* (New York: H.W. Wilson Company, 1997), p. 112.

2. Evan Thomas and Michael Hirsh, "The Future of Terror," *Newsweek*, January 10, 2000, p. 37.

3. Douglas McGray, "For Every Target, a Bomber," *Salon Magazine*, November 1, 1999, <www.salonmag. com/news/feature/1999/11/01/biowar> (July 11, 2000).

4. "Patterns of Global Terrorism: 1999," U.S. Department of State, n.d., <www.usis.usemb.se/terror/ rpt1999/review.html> (August 28, 2000).

5. Johanna McGeary, "New Year's Evil?" *Time*, December 31, 1999, p. 205, <www.time.com/time/ magazine/articles/0,3266,36512-1,00.html> (September 12, 2000).

6. "Americans Beware: Travel Carefully," ABC-NEWS.com, December 12, 1999, <abcnews.go.com/ sections/travel/DailyNews/warning_991212.html> (August 22, 2000).

7. "Report of the Accountability Review Boards," U.S. State Department, n.d.,<www.terrorism.com/ state/board_nairobi.html> (March 15, 2000)

8. Philip Shenon, "Report Calls for Closing of Vulnerable Embassies," *The New York Times*, January 9, 1999, <www.nytimes.com/library/world/africa/ 010999africa-embassy.html> (August 5, 2000).

9. "Testimony of Secretary of State Albright," Senate Budget Committee, February 11, 2000, <www. senate.gov/~budget/republican/about/hearing2000/ albright.htm> (November 17, 2000).

10. "United Nations Resolution 1267," October 15, 1999, <www.un.org/Docs/scres/1999/99sc1267.htm> (August 7, 2000).

Chapter 8. The Future of Terrorism

1. David Phinney, "The New Terrorism," ABCNews.com, n.d., <archive.abcnews.go.com/sections/us/dailyNews/terrorism_main.html> (June 28, 2000).

2. "Clinton Proposes Anti-terrorism Plan," CNN.com, January 22, 1999, <www.cnn.com/ALLPOLITICS/stories/1999/01/22/clinton.terrorism> (November 17, 2000).

3. Phinney.

4. "DOD Response to Anthrax Program Congressional Request," U.S. Department of Defense, May 16, 2000, <198.250.176.90> (November 17, 2000).

5. "Countering the Changing Threat of International Terrorism," *Report of the National Commission on Terrorism*, June 15, 2000, <www.fas.org/irp/threat/commission.html> (August 30, 2000).

6. Ibid.

7. Edward T. Pound et al., "Under Siege," *U.S. News and World Report*, September 24, 2001, pp. 14–17; "War Against Terror," CNN.com, 2001, <http://www.cnn.com/SPECIALS/2001/trade.center/victims/main.html> (October 18, 2001).

8. Ibid.

9. Michael Elliot, "'We're At War,'" *Time*, September 24, 2001, p. 40.

Glossary

al Qaeda—A terrorist group headquartered in Afghanistan and headed by Muslim extremist Osama bin Laden.

cause—A movement, usually based on political or religious ideas, to which a great many people give their support.

Central Intelligence Agency (CIA)—The U.S. government agency that uses secret agents to gather information about such things as planned terrorist attacks.

communism—A political and economic system dedicated to providing equality and security for all people based on the public, rather then private, ownership of land, factories, and other economic resources.

counterculture—A loosely based political movement from the 1960s and 1970s that opposed the basic morals and values of the existing social, political, and economic systems in the United States and some European nations.

counterterrorism—Measures taken by government authorities, such as the gathering of intelligence and the monitoring of borders, to prevent terrorism.

cult—A religious group with an extreme dedication to a leader and a set of beliefs.

detonator—A fuse or a similar device used to set off an explosive.

embassy—The official residence of an ambassador to a foreign nation and his or her staff of assistants.

ethnic—Having to do with the culture—unique customs, arts, foods, etc.—and language of large groups of people classified by common religious, racial, national, or tribal origin or background.

extremist—A person who carries his or her personal beliefs to extreme limits, such as engaging in terrorist acts in the furtherance of those beliefs.

Federal Bureau of Investigation (FBI)—The U.S. government agency responsible for preventing terrorism within U.S. borders.

forensic science—The use of scientific techniques to identify murder and disaster victims and to solve crimes.

fundamentalism—A conservative movement within a religion, such as Protestantism and Islam, based on a literal belief in religious texts, such as the Bible and the Koran.

intelligence—Information about the military, political, and economic situations of foreign nations used to keep key government officials, such as the president and Congress, informed about those nations.

Irish Republican Army (IRA)—A military organization engaging in terrorist activities that seeks to unite the independent country of Ireland with Northern Ireland, which is part of the United Kingdom.

Ku Klux Klan—A group of white secret societies that uses terrorist tactics in its opposition to African Americans, Jews, and other minority groups.

manifesto—A public announcement, usually in writing, telling of a person's or a group's purposes or motives for wanting to achieve certain goals, usually political or social in nature.

Muslims—People who practice Islam, a religion preached by the Prophet Muhammad, dating from the 7th century B.C.

National Security Agency (NSA)—The U.S. government agency that uses spy satellites and other technical devices to gather intelligence.

policy—A plan of action adopted by a government to help manage its affairs, especially with other nations.

Popular Front for the Liberation of Palestine (PFLP)— Political group founded in 1967 and operating in Syria, Lebanon, and Israel, which has conducted numerous terrorist attacks against Israel.

safe haven—An area provided for terrorists where they can safely live and plan their operations, usually provided by a government sympathetic with the terrorists' aims.

Sinn Fein—A legal political party that works on behalf of the Irish Republican Army to aid the IRA in winning independence for Northern Ireland from England.

skyjack—To take possession of a commercial airliner by force and, usually, demand that the plane be flown to a foreign country and the passengers and crew held for ransom.

state-sponsored terrorism—The practice of governments actively supporting terrorist groups by supplying them with money, weapons, and places to live.

terrorism—The unlawful use of force or violence against persons or property to intimidate or coerce a government, the civilian population, or any segment thereof, in furtherance of political or social objectives.

terrorist—A person who uses or favors terrorism.

vehicle identification number (VIN)—A seventeen-character code number printed on the dashboard or driver's side door post of a vehicle that, when decoded, gives information about the vehicle such as year, make, body style, and engine size.

weapons of mass destruction (WMD)—Chemical, biological, and nuclear weapons with the power to kill vast numbers of people and make entire regions of the world uninhabitable.

Further Reading

Andryszewski, Tricia. *The Militia Movement in America: Before & After Oklahoma City.* Brookfield, Conn.: Millbrook Press, 1997.

Brennan, Jill W. *Terrorism: Threat & Response.* Kettering, Ohio: PPI Publishing, 1992.

Dumas, Alexander. *Lethal Arrogance.* New York: St. Martin's Press, 1999.

Egendorf, Laura K. *Terrorism.* San Diego, Calif.: Greenhaven Press, Inc., 1999.

McGuckin, Frank (ed). *Terrorism in the United States.* New York: H.W. Wilson Company, 1997.

Streissguth, Tom. *International Terrorists.* Minneapolis, Minn.: Oliver Press, Inc., 1999.

Waits, Chris and David Shors. *Unabomber: The Secret Life of Ted Kaczynski.* Helena, Mont.: American World Geographic Publishing, 1999.

Internet Addresses

The Central Intelligence Agency (CIA)

<http://www.cia.gov>

This government agency is responsible for gathering information from around the world about matters that affect national security. Use the site's search for an extensive list of articles about international terrorism.

The Federal Bureau of Investigation (FBI)

<http://www.fbi.gov>

This government agency shares responsibility with the CIA for gathering information about matters affecting national security. The FBI is also responsible for actively combatting terrorist acts.

The National Institute of Justice
<http://www.ojp.usdoj.gov/nij/about.htm>
This is the research agency of the U.S. Department of Justice. It handles research on criminal behavior and crime prevention, including terrorism. Use this site's search engine for research articles about terrorism.

The Oklahoma City National Memorial
<http://www.oklahomacitynationalmemorial.org>
The memorial, dedicated to the victims of the Oklahoma City bombing, was dedicated on April 19, 2000. A description of the memorial and a map of how to reach it can be found at the official memorial Web site.

The Terrorism Research Center
<http://www.terrorism.com/index.shtml>
This Web site is dedicated to informing the public about the phenomenon of terrorism. It features essays and speeches on current issues, as well as profiles of terrorist groups and counterterrorism organizations.

The U.S. Information Agency Terrorism Issues Page
<http://usinfo.state.gov/topical/pol/terror>
This U.S. government-sponsored site includes official government documents on terrorism and special reports on current events involving terrorism.

U.S. State Department: Office of the Coordinator for Counterterrorism
<http://www.state.gov/s/ct/>
This is the official Web site of the coordinator of U.S. counterterrorism efforts. It includes annual reports on terrorism around the world.

Index